MUSTANG

FOUR DECADES OF MUSCLE CAR POWER

CRESTLINE

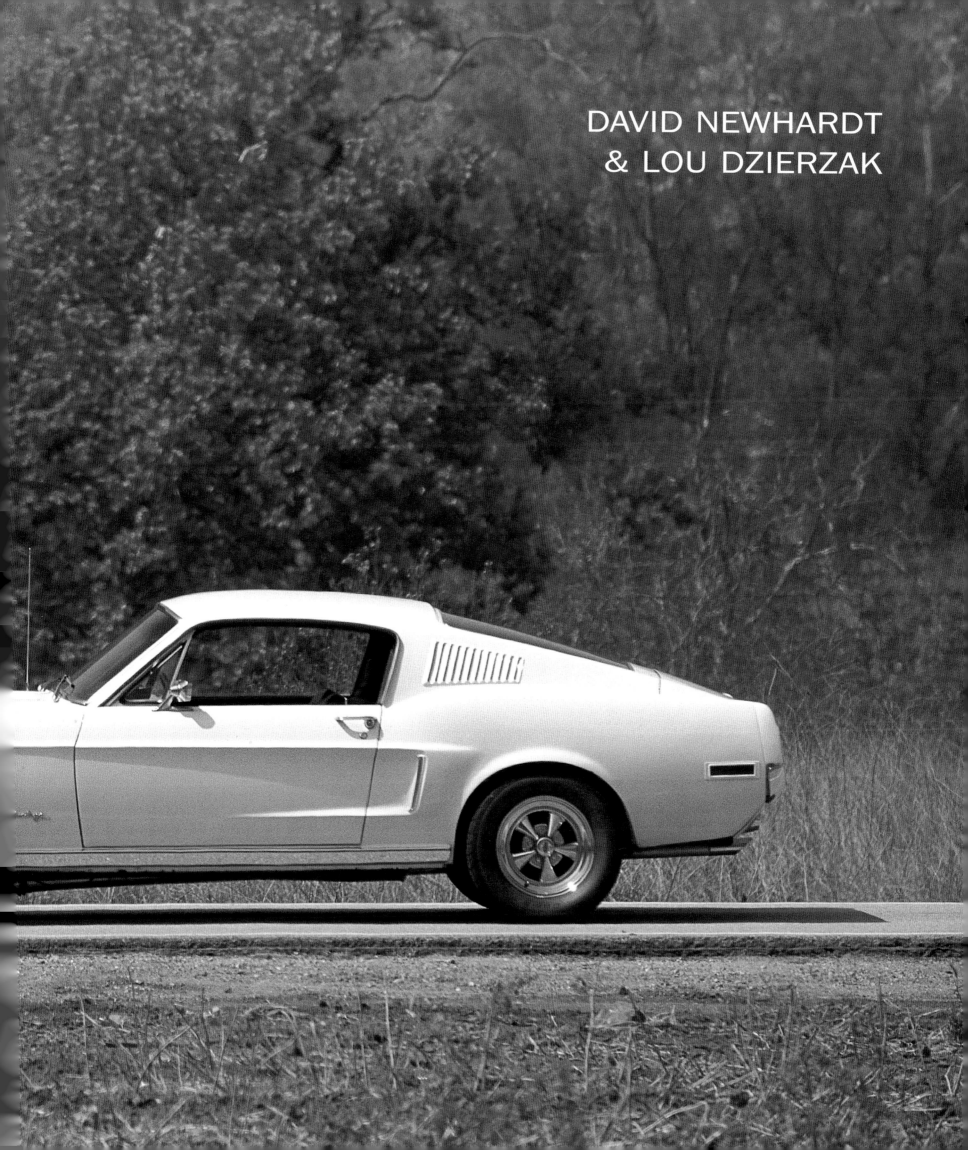

DAVID NEWHARDT
& LOU DZIERZAK

First published in 2003 by Motorbooks International, an imprint of MBI Publishing
Company, Galtier Plaza, Suite 200, 380 Jackson Street, St. Paul, MN 55101-3885 USA

All photography by David Newhardt unless otherwise noted.

The information in this book is true and complete to the best of our knowledge.
All recommendations are made without any guarantee on the part of the author or
Publisher, who also disclaim any liability incurred in connection with the use of this
data or specific details.

We recognize that some words, model names and designations, for example, mentioned
herein are the property of the trademark holder. We use them for identification purposes
only. This is not an official publication.

Motorbooks International titles are also available at discounts in bulk quantity for
industrial or sales-promotional use. For details write to Special Sales Manager at
Motorbooks International Wholesalers & Distributors, Galtier Plaza, Suite 200,
380 Jackson Street, St. Paul, MN 55101-3885 USA.

ISBN 0-7603-1731-3

Edited by: Amy Glaser
Designed by: Katie Sonmor
Cover design: Koechel-Peterson & Associates, Minneapolis, Minnesota

Printed in China

CONTENTS

Acknowledgments

In 2004, Ford will celebrate the 40th anniversary of the Mustang. From the original pony car introduced at the World's Fair in New York to the automotive press to conjecture about the look of the next generation Mustang there is a story to tell about each and ever model. Names like Shelby, Cobra, Boss, Mach 1, and Bullitt bring back memories of a time when performance was measured by 0 to 60 and the time needed to cover a quarter-mile.

MBI Publishing Company has published a series of books that tell the Mustang's story from every possible point of view. This book would not exist without the hard work, dedication, and passion of the writers who told the story before me.

My thanks to Bill Coulter, Tom Corcoran, Randy Leffingwell, Mike Mueller, David Newhardt, Peter Sessler, and Matt Stone for providing me with a place to start.

Words alone can't describe the sleek lines, powerful engines, and fine design details of the Mustang. The photographers in this book have truly captured its essence. Turn the pages a little slower and lose yourself in the images. Imagine yourself behind the wheel. Thanks to David Newhardt and Bill Coulter for bringing these Mustang stories to life.

At MBI, my thanks to editor Josh Leventhal for giving me the opportunity to write this book. Amy Glaser guided the book through its final stages with grace, patience, and boundless energy. Thanks Amy.

Finally, thanks to my family. Taylor, thank you for listening to me recite the details of every Mustang we passed on the road. Claire, thanks for being patient with me every time I said, "In a few minutes." Carey, thanks for making my dreams come true.

A 1999 Mustang SVO.

Introduction

On April 17, 1964, Lee Iacocca and the Ford Motor Company introduced a new kind of car to a generation of young adults with money to spend and a need to express themselves through their clothes, music, and especially their cars.

The Mustang has become an American icon for nearly 40 years. The preintroduction buzz of the first Mustang was so high that 22,000 Mustangs were sold the first day. Ford offered car enthusiasts more choices than ever before. Depending on the buyer, the first generation Mustang was an economical commuter, a wind-in-your-hair luxury convertible, or a flat-out high-performance street racer.

Change comes once a year in the automotive world. Each fall a new Mustang was unveiled. From the heady days of the 1960s to the energy crisis of the 1970s and prosperity of the 1990s, the evolution of the Mustang reflects the history of American culture.

The first generation of the Mustang ran from 1964 to 1973. With models like the Boss 302, Mach I and GT, the Mustang set a high standard for performance cars. The second generation (1974–1978) are not remembered fondly by Mustang enthusiasts, but remember the times. Federal emission standards, safety regulations, and skyrocketing insurance premiums spelled the end of the performance era for all American car manufacturers.

Ford reinvented the Mustang in 1979. The third generation took on a look and personality of its own. It was chosen as the official pace car of the 1979 Indianapolis 500, and the new Mustang wore the galloping pony badge with pride.

A new standard of performance returned with the introduction of the

1994 Cobra.

5.0 liter engine and Ford's Special Vehicle Operation modified Mustangs. Sophisticated new engines, performance suspension packages and aerodynamic bodies helped the Cobra, GT, and SVO Mustangs live up to the performance image created by the first generation.

The fourth generation was introduced in 1994 and reflected the long hood, short rear deck body of the first pony car. The Special Vehicle Team Cobra featured a coiled snake badge reminiscent of the Shelby Cobras sold 30 years earlier.

Today, as anticipation for the next generation builds, the Mustang has millions of fans with stories to tell about their own cars and experiences. Collectors chase stories of pristine limited edition models stored in barns, websites devoted to Mustangs share the love and books like this try to capture the spirit of the car. I hope this book rekindles your own memories and recollections.

1966 Mustang.

The 1960s
Mustang Roots

In May 1962, Lee Iacocca directed a group of Ford engineers to build a show car demonstrating the "Total Performance—Powered by Ford" concept.

The team worked night and day to design and build the car and was ready to introduce the car 22 weeks later. On October 7, Ford executives and engineers rolled the mystery car out of a transporter at the Watkins Glen racetrack.

The low, sleek, white Mustang I was constructed of a welded tubular steel space frame. The interior featured fixed bucket seats. The seat frames contributed to the chassis' strength. To accommodate a range of drivers, the steering column and foot pedals could be moved forward to back up to four inches. Although it was a concept car, the instrument panel was nicely finished and complete. A V-4 engine with a front trans-axle originally slated for another Ford car was used to power the Mustang I. At the rear, the twin exhaust pipes exited through the fiberglass body. John Najjar, one of the designers on the project, suggested the Mustang name based on his interest in the World War II P-51 combat fighter.

To generate interest in the Total Performance concept, Ford took the Mustang I on tour to visit major auto shows across the country. Two cars were built; one was completely road-worthy, and the second was just a shell for photography. Recruiting college engineers was a key part of the tour, with Ford managers making stops at 17 mechanical and engineering schools.

Although the Mustang I generated a buzz in the trade press and among the automobile enthusiasts who saw the car, Ford management didn't move forward with production. Lee Iacocca turned his sights to a four-seater he had in mind.

5-25-62
S-5439-7

With Iacocca in charge of Ford, the push towards "Total Performance" took shape with the design of the Mustang I in 1962, a mid-engine, two-seater.

The Mustang I of 1962 used an aluminum body fitted over a tube frame built up using 1-inch tubing. Large scoops on the side allowed cooling air to flow into the German V-4's radiators.

Adjustable pedals and steering column meant that drivers of various sizes could get comfortable in the fixed bucket seats. Bullet-shaped pods on the dash held a full slate of instruments.

Lee Iacocca—Father of the Mustang

A recent Princeton engineering grad, Lee Iacocca joined the Ford Motor Company in 1946 when he was 22 years old. Iacocca was hired as an engineering trainee yet found himself more suited to the sales side of the company. His innovative sales ideas sold cars, and he succeeded Robert McNamara as vice president and general manager in 1960.

Intrigued with demographic information that forecasted a dramatic increase in young car buyers with money in their pockets, Iacocca led the charge to build a small, sporty car. In his view, the car needed to seat four, be fun to drive, and affordable.

Iacocca assembled a team of designers, engineers, and marketers to bring the idea to life. The group, named the Fairlane Committee, initially met to brainstorm all aspects of the new car. Iacocca swore the team to secrecy and even burned notes taken at the meetings. After long nights and great debate, the team had its plan for an affordable sports car.

In September 1962, Iacocca approached Henry Ford II and made his pitch. Ford listened to Iacocca's market research data, engineering cost analysis, and a dramatically new car design and approved a $40 million budget to build the new sporty car Iacocca was so passionately dedicated to building. If the pace was fast before that meeting, it certainly picked up afterwards. The new car was set for introduction March 1964, less than 18 months away from the approval date.

Inside Ford, the car was still being called the Cougar, Special Falcon, or the T-5. Ford stylist John Najjar, inspired by the P-51 Mustang fighter bomber that was flown in World War II, suggested the new car carry the same name.

As part of its role to develop marketing campaigns for new Ford cars and trucks, Ford's advertising agency, J. W. Thompson, was asked to develop a list of names for the new car. The agency's initial list contained 6,000 names. The final six were: Cougar, Bronco, Puma, Cheetah, Colt, and Mustang. From November 1962 forward, the new two-seater was called Mustang. During the approval process, the Mustang changed from an airplane to a horse. Designer Phil Clark drew the original galloping horse logo.

On March 11, 1964, William B. Ford III, Henry Ford II's nephew, spent his lunch hour driving a preproduction black Mustang convertible around downtown Dearborn. *Detroit Free Press* employee Fred Olmstead spotted the car and called a staff photographer. The news was out. The buzz began. Ford was ready to introduce something radically different.

On April 17, 1964 Lee Iacocca stood center stage at the New York World's Fair and officially introduced the Mustang to a crowd of reporters and car buffs.

The pre-release publicity campaign was so successful Ford dealers were packed the next day. With a base price of $2,368, the Mustang exceeded Iacocca's most optimistic sales objectives. Twenty-two thousand were sold the first day and almost 700,000 were sold by August 1965.

In large part because of the Mustang's success, Iacocca moved up the ladder to become executive vice president in charge of North American Operations and ready to make a move for the top spot at Ford. In 1970, Henry Ford II fired Bunkie Knudsen and named Iacocca president of Ford Motor Company.

Times had changed since the introduction of the first Mustang. Gasoline prices were soaring, and America's love of high-performance cars was replaced with a call for value, fuel economy, and comfort.

Once again, Iacocca led the engineering, design, and marketing teams to create the Mustang II. Supported with design input from Ghia of Italy, the new Mustang was smaller, lighter, and more luxurious than models from the previous years.

Iacocca wanted the new Mustang II to be perceived as a comfortable mini limousine. It was the first car equipped with an American built metric four-cylinder engine. Unfortunately, the introduction of the Mustang II didn't go as well as the Mustang I. Sales at the end of 30 days totaled 18,000; 4,000 less than the original Mustang sold in its first day. A few years later, in 1978, the father of the Mustang was fired. Shortly after, Iacocca joined Chrysler and continued his successful approach to sales there.

1964-1/2
Mustang Convertible

Some books and resources list the first Mustang as a 1964-1/2 model. For the record, Ford management never referred to the original car this way. Mustangs built between March 1964 and August 1964 were called early 1965 models. Those built after August 17, 1964, were called late 1965s.

Early Mustangs used a generator, and models built after August 1964 used an alternator. The wiring for each version was different. Mustangs with generators came with a "GEN" warning light on the instrument panel. Alternator-equipped models had an "ALT" warning light.

The Mustang was based on the Ford Falcon unibody platform. The design elements that will always make Mustang distinctive is a long hood, sculptured side panels, and a short rear deck. The fastback body style was introduced in September 1964.

Ford could barely keep up with the pace of sales. Demand outstripped production capacity. Initially built in Dearborn, Michigan, Ford shifted additional production to plants in San Jose, California, and Metuchen, New Jersey.

As the Mustangs rolled off the assembly line, running changes were made in standard equipment and options, such as chrome-plated door locks. On early models, the buttons were color-matched to the interior. The spacing between the Mustang letters on the body side nameplate was lengthened to five inches.

By the end of 1964, Ford had sold 263,434 Mustangs. On the

1964-1/2 Mustang

first anniversary, Ford had established a new single year sales record with 417,471 sold.

The Mustang's original base engine was the 170-ci six or the 260-ci V-8. In the fall of 1964, the 200-ci six and 289 V-8 became the standard powerplants.

To add more power and performance, a 164 horsepower, 260-ci V-8 and a 210 horsepower, 289-ci V-8 were available engine options. A 271 horsepower 289 was added after June 1, 1964.

At the factory, six-cylinder engines were painted red, and V-8 engines were painted black with gold air cleaners and valve covers.

The standard transmission was a four-speed manual. A special handling package included stiffer shocks and springs with 14-inch tires and wheels. Firestone Super Sport tires were optional.

1991 Mustang SVO.

Mustang Marketing

After several years of nonstop debate, planning, and engineering trial and error, Ford management wanted to create a buzz about their new car. In late 1963, Ford invited writers and editors from top magazines like *Time*, *Newsweek*, *Life*, *Look*, *Esquire*, and *Sports Illustrated* to Dearborn, Michigan, to hear presentations about a new style of car.

Press kits were mailed to another 11,000 newspaper and magazine writers. To cover the airwaves, Ford invited almost 200 of the best known disc jockeys for a sneak peak at Dearborn just a few weeks before the unveiling.

On April 13, 1964, more than 125 reporters gathered to hear Ford Vice President Lee Iacocca talk about the growing youth market and finally introduce the most anticipated car in decades.

Later that afternoon, Ford handed car keys to a select group of reporters. The 150 car caravan drove 750 miles from New York to Dearborn, turning heads every mile along the way.

That evening, Walter Hoving, chairman of Tiffany and Company, presented Henry Ford II with the Tiffany Gold Medal "for excellence in American design." The inscription read, "Mustang has the look, the fire and flavor of one of the great European road cars. Yet it is as American as its name and as practical as its price." The Ford Mustang was the first automobile to receive the honor.

The carefully orchestrated marketing campaign took another step on April 16. At 9:30 P.M., Mustang commercials ran on all three television networks simultaneously. An ad in that week's issue of *TV Guide* promised, "the most exciting thing on TV tonight will be a commercial." Nielsen ratings reported that over 29 million people were introduced to the Mustang that night. Over the next week, Ford Mustang commercials ran in 32 different programs and 52 minutes of selling time. They were featured prizes on the ABC's *The Price is Right* and NBC's *Word for Word*, *Concentration*, and *Let's Make a Deal*.

The day after the television blitz, Ford placed newspaper ads in 2,600 newspapers and 24 national magazines. Lee Iacocca and the Mustang appeared on the covers of *Time* and *Newsweek*, and magazines as varied as *Businessweek*, *Sports Illustrated*, *Look*, *Popular Science*, and *Playboy* ran feature stories on the new pony car.

Ford provided dealers with its advertising plans to introduce the new Mustang. Although the dealers had some advance notice, no one was ready for the public's response to the marketing campaign. Enthusiastic car buyers placed 22,000 orders the first day. Dealers were overwhelmed with the response. Ford used an official "Mustang Order Holding" form that helped the dealer close the sale. Customers who were patient enough to wait for their Mustang received two special gifts. The first 50,000 buyers who completed the form received a scale model Mustang, a personalized "Original Edition

Mustang" nameplate, and a selection of gift cards. Dealers were charged $2 per order.

Iacocca's goal for the introduction was to break the Falcon's record for new model first year sales. The rallying cry at the Ford offices was 417 by 4-17; to sell 417,000 Mustangs by the first anniversary of the introduction.

The goal was achieved. Barely. On April 17, 1965, the records showed Ford sold 418,812 Mustangs—1,638 more than the previous record set by the 1960 Falcon.

Mustang's First Official Owner

Two weeks before the Mustang's spectacular debut, 33-year-old Captain Stanley Tucker, an Eastern Provincial Airlines pilot from St. John's spotted a Mustang convertible at his hometown dealership, George Parsons Ford. The car had been on tour throughout Canada to generate preintroduction interest. Captain Tucker saw the Wimbledon White Mustang, bought it on the spot, and became the first owner anywhere in North America. His car carried the serial number 100001. Ford officials had planned to bring the car home and display it in the company museum; Captain Stanley had other ideas. He refused to sell the car back to Ford. Ford officials continued to negotiate, and two years later, a deal was struck. If Captain Stanley agreed to return the first Mustang, he would be given one carrying serial number 1,000,001 with anything he wanted on it.

When the one millionth Mustang rolled off the assembly line, Captain Tucker traded in his slightly used Mustang with 10,000 miles on the odometer for a fully loaded 1966 convertible painted in Silver Frost with a Deluxe black interior. His equipment package included the 289 4V engine, Cruise-O-Matic transmission, air conditioning, disc brakes, a Stereosonic tape player, Rally-Pac, and styled steel wheels. Captain Tucker drove the car in Canada and on the Caribbean Island of Antigua. He sold it five years later.

The first Mustang now resides in the Henry Ford Museum in Dearborn, Michigan. The fate of the one millionth Mustang is unknown.

The 1965 Mustang coupe was officially introduced on October 1, 1964. Model year production totaled 559,451. The 2+2 two-door fastback coupe was added in September 1964. All three body styles were offered until 1973. The 1965 coupe outsold the other body styles by a wide margin. Almost 75 percent of Mustangs sold in 1965 were hardtops.

The options available that year included power brakes, manual front disc brakes, power steering, limited slip differential, styled steel wheels, underdash air conditioner, and a vinyl roof. The average buyer added $1,000 in options to the $2,386 base price.

The interior also received special treatment. The Interior Décor Group was introduced in March 1965. Deluxe door panels, special upholstery with galloping pony inserts, woodgrain steering wheel, woodgrain appliques on the glove box door, and a special five-dial instrument cluster were some of the new luxury interior additions.

Mustangs were selling as fast as the factories could build them, but car enthusiasts begged for more performance. Ford responded by introducing two options. The Mustang GT was introduced on April 17, 1965. The Shelby Mustangs were even more powerful.

GT Equipment Group

This performance package was available on all three body styles. The package included manual front disc brakes, quick ratio steering, dual exhaust with chrome exhaust tips, rocker panel stripes, GT emblems, and two fog lamps mounted in the grille opening.

On the GT, the instrument panel was upgraded with a five dial version—fuel, temperature, speed, oil pressure, and amps.

In the base model, the GT was powered with the 225 horsepower, 289 four-barrel V-8. The 289 High Performance V-8, 271 horsepower engine was the only available option. A three-speed transmission was standard on all GT models.

The majority of 1965 Mustang GTs packed the 280-ci A-code V-8 engine. With its durable iron block and heads, it made 225 horsepower.

Buyers wanting to perk-up the interior of their 1965 Mustang GT might order the $107.08 Interior Décor Group, commonly called the Pony Interior due to the embossing on the seat backs.

Ideal for wide-open roads, the 1965 Mustang convertible K-code was the hottest version of the marque, with its 289-ci V-8 delivering a healthy 271 horsepower. The folding top was electrically operated.

1965

Grille-mounted fog lamps were standard
with the GT package, a mandatory option
when ordering the 271 horsepower K-code.
Doorsill stripes mimicked the Mustang's
Shelby cousin.

Ordering a K-code Mustang in 1965 meant a four-speed manual transmission, period. A stylish center console was a $50.41 option.

Fastback models enjoyed a folding rear seat that transformed the diminutive bench into a commodious storage area.

A styling line on the side of the 1965 Mustang hinted at the functional side air inlets on the 1962 Mustang engineering study. The simulated scoop continues to the present day.

Carroll Shelby and Ford Mustang

From the beginning, the 1964 Ford Mustang was a great sales success. Although the pony car looked sporty enough, Ford wanted to compete on the same performance level as the Corvette.

Texan Carroll Shelby, well-known for his racing prowess, was forced to stop driving due to a heart condition. Shelby applied his skills and experience to a driving school and the development of the AC Cobra. The success of that car led to Shelby's five-year-long relationship with Ford.

Ford pulled partially built Mustang fastbacks from the San Jose assembly plant and shipped them to Shelby's small factory near the Los Angeles airport.

Shelby and his team began the modification process and added a four-speed transmission to the 271 horsepower High Performance 289 V-8. The engine received upgraded parts like aluminum valve covers, a high-rise intake manifold, and a Holley carburetor.

From the start, Ford wanted the Shelby Mustangs to be performance stars. The first step was to build cars for the Sports Car Club of America (SCCA) racing circuit. In order to qualify as an SCCA B-Production racer, the organizing body required the manufacturer to build at least 100 street models.

With long hours, hard work, and a little luck, Shelby met the deadline. Shelby's Venice, California, factory turned out several hundred hand-assembled cars each month. The GT 350R model was race ready and brought trophies home right away.

Over the next five years, Shelby Mustang scored victories in many events including Daytona, Sebring, and Le Mans.

Two years after the first Shelby Mustang appeared, car buyers demanded bigger engines with more power. Shelby responded by increasing the size of the GT 350 engine and introduced the GT 500 with the 428 engine.

By 1969, Ford was offering its own performance models like the Boss 302 and 429, and the relationship came to a close. To this day, Shelby Mustangs are highly sought after by performance car collectors.

1965
Shelby GT 350

The Shelby GT line began with the GT 350. In 1965, 562 GT 350s were produced. Since the cars were built by hand, minor variations in parts and assembly techniques were common throughout the production run. The 516 street models were expensive at $4,547, and the remaining 36 received the R designation for road racing editions.

Performance enthusiasts took one look at this car and knew it was special. White with a wide Guardsman Blue racing stripe, the first Shelby model was identified by the GT 350 decal on the rocker panel and at the right rear panel between the fuel cap and the taillight.

The fiberglass hood of the Shelby Mustang was equipped with a functional hood scoop. The Mustang logo was moved to the driver's side of the black honeycomb, mesh screen grille.

The Shelby interior used the Mustang's Falcon-style instrument cluster, upholstery, door panels, and black carpeting. The instrument panel included a tachometer and oil pressure gauge. The horn wasn't included in the steering wheel. The driver flipped a switch on the dashboard to activate it. Since it was a performance car, three-inch-wide competition lap belts were installed. Their attachment points connected to the drive-shaft safety loop under the car.

Wooden steering wheels were a common design element on Shelbys. The first 100 cars came with a 16-inch wheel with slotted spokes. Later production cars came with 15-inch wheels with slotted spokes.

The engine was the stock High Performance 271 horsepower 289. Shelby modified the engine with an aluminum high rise intake manifold, a Holley four-barrel carburetor, and steel headers. Pipes exited just in front of the rear wheels. The changes boosted the horsepower to 306. The engine was dressed up with finned cast-aluminum valve covers with "Cobra Powered by Ford" lettering.

The 1965 GT 350 R-model was meant strictly for track use. Although only 36 were built, their dominance in SCCA racing resulted in valuable press coverage that far out weighed their numbers.

Using a molded front fiberglass apron to replace the steel bumper shaved weight and allowed improved airflow through the radiator. SCCA rules allowed the removal of rear bumper entirely.

LEFT: At home on the street as well as a racetrack, the 1965 Shelby GT 350 was a shrewd marketing move by both Ford and Shelby. Ford basked in the reflected glow of the GT 350s racing successes, and Shelby just sold a lot of cars.

Functional air extraction louvers on the 1965 Mustang's C-pillars were carried over to the GT 350 of that year. Wide, competition grade seat belts were standard in the Shelby.

Demand for a performance Mustang was answered with the introduction of the K-code option in 1965. Equipped with a 271 horsepower V-8 and a sport suspension, it was the basis for Shelby's GT 350.

Exhaust pipes exited in front of the rear tires, which was a common racing trick to minimize back pressure and save weight. Its timeless proportions are evident in the profile.

Taking Mustang shells from the Ford assembly line, craftsmen created a hairy-chested sports car at Shelby American's plant in Los Angeles. Side C-scoop was put to good use on future Shelby Mustangs.

After the amazing success of the 1965 Mustang, only minor styling changes were made. The front grille was changed to a floating Mustang emblem with no horizontal or vertical dividing bars.

The 1966 Mustang was offered in a coupe, convertible, and fastback body style. Sales continued to match the record-setting pace of 1965. In fact, the 1966 coupe holds the honor of the best-selling Mustang model ever.

Early Mustangs offered buyers a wide range of option packages. Owners could select complete groups or pick selected options and build their own one-of-a-kind Mustang. The Deluxe Interior Group featured embossed galloping horses on the upper sections of the seat backs.

Beginning in 1966, Mustang offered an AM/FM radio option. Since FM broadcasting wasn't widespread until the end of the decade, the option was priced at almost twice the amount of the AM-only radio.

Mustangs came with 14x4.5-inch wheels. The six-cylinder models had four lug nuts, and the V-8 came with five lug nuts. Whitewalls were optional. The standard wheel cover was redesigned, and the optional styled steel wheels featured a chrome trim ring.

The first year of federally mandated safety standards was 1966. Standard safety equipment on all Fords included front and rear seat belts, padded instrument panel, emergency flashers, electric wipers, and windshield washers. The five-dial instrument panel became standard across all Mustang models.

The model year production reached 607,586. Representing over 7 percent of all American cars sold, the Mustang was the third best-selling individual nameplate that year. It was amazing for a model that was only three years old.

To commemorate the sale of one millionth Mustang, Ford introduced the Sprint 200 Option Group. Available on the hardtop, convertible, and fastback, it consisted of the 200 V-6 engine, wire wheel covers, pinstripes, center console, and a chrome air cleaner.

The T-5

Ford sold cars throughout Europe. Ford wanted to sell the Mustang to American military servicemen and local car enthusiasts in Germany. However, a West German manufacturer, Humbold-Klockner-Dautz, owned the rights to the word Mustang.

The company offered to sell the Mustang naming rights to Ford for $10,000, but officials in Dearborn declined. Ford removed all the Mustang badges and emblems and renamed the car the T-5. The Mustang badge on the front fender panel was replaced with a horizontal T-5 badge. The galloping pony on stripes crest on the steering wheel hub was the only clue to the T-5's American roots. The T-5 model was sold from 1964 to 1974.

Horizontal grille bars were one on the few stylistic changes in 1966. The vee emblem on the tip of the front fenders indicated a V-8 under the long hood.

Ford offered a Mustang Sprint in 1966, consisting of a 200-ci, straight six-cylinder engine.
With 120 horsepower, the emphasis was on economy, not neck-snapping performance.

Long hood/short trunk proportions found on the Mustang became the signature style for pony cars, so-named after the Mustang.

All Mustangs came with the five-pod instrument cluster in 1966. Air conditioning was a $310.90 option, with the louvers and controls located in a large pod mounted under the center of the dashboard.

America was not the only country that sold Mustangs. In West Germany, Ford's pony was called the T-5.

On T-5s bound for West Germany, Ford installed this badge on the glove box door to replace the Mustang emblem found on American cars.

A rose by any other name.... The only difference between European and American Mustangs is the absence of Mustang badging on the European version.

Shelby GT 350 Racing

The Shelby GT 350R racing models were equipped with a fiberglass front lower fender apron, engine oil cooler, larger capacity radiator, front and rear brake cooling assemblies, 34-gallon fuel tank, 3-1/2 quick fill gas cap, electric fuel pump, and large diameter exhaust pipes with no muffler. The curb weight was 2,790 pounds. Shelby Racing models won the B-production championship in 1965, 1966, and 1967.

1966 Shelby GT 350

The first 262 cars of 1966 Shelby GT 350 model production were actually leftover 1965s that were upgraded to 1966 specifications. Changes for the second model year included new louvers on the rear window pillar with Plexiglas windows, and a rear seat replaced the original models fiberglass shelf. According to production records, 82 cars were sold with fold-down rear seats.

Shelby American built six convertibles at the end of 1966, but none were sold to the public. Shelby awarded the convertibles to hard-working employees and business associates. All six were painted different colors and equipped with automatic transmissions and air conditioning. Including the Hertz cars, 2,380 Shelby GTs were produced in 1966.

Hertz

Shelby American General Manager Peyton Cramer approached Hertz in September 1965 to offer them a special edition of the GT 350. Hertz agreed in principle, and after a series of prototypes were delivered in October and November, Hertz ordered 1,000 cars in late December.

The special editions were painted black with gold stripes. According to Shelby American Automotive Club records, 75 percent of the Hertz cars were black with gold stripes. Hertz GT 350H models came with standard black upholstery, three-inch wide seat belts, front disc brakes, and dash mounted tachometers. Other modifications included Magnum steel wheels with Goodyear Blue Streak tires.

Hertz charged Sports Car Club members $17 a day and 17 cents per mile to drive the rent-a-racer. Hertz included Shelby cars in their fleet again in 1968 and 1969, but the second generation cars did not have the GT 350H emblem.

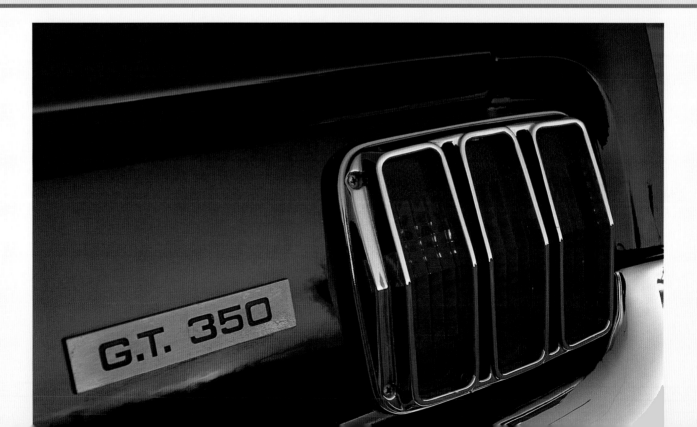

One of the few external changes on the GT 350 for 1966 was the replacement of the C-pillar louvers with a lightweight Plexiglas window, cutting weight, and improving outward visibility.

For the first couple of years, Shelby utilized standard Mustang taillights and affixed a badge to the rear panel to differentiate the GT 350 from the Mustang.

Unlike the molded pod used to house the tachometer and oil pressure gauge in 1965, the 1966 GT 350 bolted the tach on top of the dash. The oil pressure gauge was now found in the instrument cluster.

Few exterior changes were made on the Shelby GT 350H, primarily the fitting of the Bronze Metallic stripes. A discreet identification badge next to the taillight was sufficient to impress the informed.

A functional air scoop fed outside air into the engine compartment. The air cleaner element is visible, peeking through the opening.

Rocker panel stripes on the 1966 Shelby GT 350H denoted a Hertz Rent-A-Car. Shelby built 1,000 in 1966, contributing about 40 percent to the year's total production.

Shelby mounted the vehicle identification tag on top of the standard Mustang VIN atop the left fender. A first digit of six denotes this Shelby as a 1966 model.

1967

The Mustang was completely redesigned in 1967. Everything became bigger. The exterior dimensions said the Mustang was longer and wider than the year before. Underneath the body, the chassis, frame structure, and running gear remained unchanged.

The grille featured a larger openings and the size of the non-functional air scoop on the side was also increased. At the rear, the taillight design shifted to three vertical lenses on each side of a concave panel. The pop-open gas cap was located in the center.

Engine options remained the same as 1966 except for the introduction of the 390 big block with a single Holley carburetor and cast-iron intake and exhaust manifolds.

The engine was big, heavy, and made for low-end torque and performance. Called the Thunderbird Special, the 390 featured a hydraulic camshaft and a Holley four-barrel carburetor. The 390 was made for acceleration. Mustangs equipped with the 390 could reach 0 to 60 in just over seven seconds. Equipped with a four-speed manual transmission, the 390 could cover a quarter-mile in about 15 seconds. All 390s used a dual exhaust system.

For the racer, Ford offered the Competition Handling Package to supplement the 390 engine. Priced at $388.53, the package included upgraded springs, Gabriel shocks, quick ratio steering, front sway bar, limited slip axle, and 15-inch steel wheels with wire wheel covers.

The Exterior Décor Group package was offered for the first time in 1967. Elements included a hood with rear facing louvers that housed turn-signal indicator lights, wheel well moldings, and a pop-open gas cap.

While the 1967 Mustang used the same 108-inch wheelbase as years before, the sheet metal grew to allow larger engines. Mustangs were popular recipients of aftermarket wheels.

GT model Mustangs carried fog lamps inside of the grille. Air vents behind the doors were for show only. This style was found on 1967 Mustangs only.

A rarely seen factory option is the lower back panel grille, a $19.48 dress-up part seen on this 1967 hardtop. Dual exhausts with quad chrome exhaust tips were part of the $205.05 GT option.

Dealer-installed options flourished as buyers strived to differentiate their Mustangs from the hundreds of thousands sold. One such item was the illuminated pony in the grille that glowed when the headlights were on.

By 1967, the Mustang could be ordered with an increasing number of comfort and convenience options, including a tilt-away steering wheel and a reverb control mounted underneath the glove box.

The clean roofline introduced on the 1965 Mustang was retained on the first restyle of the pony car for 1967. While the wheelbase remained the same at 108 inches, the overall length increased.

1967
Shelby GT 350 & GT 500

Two Shelby models were sold in 1967: the GT 350 with the High Performance 289 V-8 and the GT 500 with the 428-ci V-8. Built to go fast, the redesigned Shelbys looked fast standing still. The rear window pillar was changed to add a scoop that moved air to the back seat passengers. Early production models included a small red light, but federal regulations caused Shelby to remove the light for the remainder of the year.

Fiberglass hood and body panels were used to differentiate Shelby models from standard Mustang fastbacks and GT models. A three-inch hood extension topped a special grille that contained two seven-inch driving lights. In most models, the lights are mounted in the center of the grille. After complaints from several states, the lights were moved farther apart.

In 1967, all Shelby models came equipped with the Mustang Deluxe interior that featured special upholstery and molded seatbacks, fold-down rear seats, brushed aluminum insets, and door trim pieces.

As Shelby used the Mustang as the base for its upgrades, the 1967 GT 350 and big-block GT 500 grew as well. Very few GT 350s were fitted with the Paxton supercharger option, adding another 100 horsepower to the 306 horsepower 289-ci V-8.

Side scoops on Shelbys were functional. The C-pillar scoops pulled air from the interior, while the lower scoops directed cool air to the rear brakes.

GT 500

The GT 500 came with a modified version of Ford's 428-ci Police Interceptor V-8. The powerful engine came with two Holley carburetors and an aluminum intake manifold. An oval Cobra finned air cleaner matched the Cobra finned valve covers. The big block engine filled the engine compartment with no room to spare.

The Shelby GT 500 was the only Mustang model to come equipped with the 428 engine. Standard Mustangs would wait until 1968 for this engine option. Ford conservatively rated the 428 at 355 horsepower. Performance shops boosted that to over 400 horsepower. In 1967 Ford sold 3,225 Shelby Mustangs, which was an increase of 50 percent over 1966.

Taillights sourced from the 1967 Cougar without the chrome trim flanked a pop-open gas cap. Shelby had access to Ford's part bin, which was helpful in styling a different look while holding down costs.

Center-mounted high-beam headlights ran afoul of a handful of state regulations, forcing Shelby to move the lights to the outboard edges of the grille. One result was improved engine cooling.

Shelby "borrowed" the Cobra emblem from his two-seat models and used them on the Mustang-derived GT models. Rocker stripes were styled by Peter Brock, Carroll Shelby's first employee.

Ten-spoke aluminum wheels and the aggressive profile, including the lengthened nose and Kamm-inspired tail spoiler, were standard on Shelby GT models.

1968
Shelby GT 500KR

Shelby did not go to great lengths in 1968 to change its design from the prior year. A revised hood, with air inlets on the leading edge and air extraction louvers at the back, was the most visible difference.

Shelby production continued at the A.O. Smith Company facility in Livonia, Michigan. For the first time, the public could buy a convertible version of the GT 350 or GT 500. The body styles were similar between 1966 and 1968. The fiberglass nose was restyled in 1968 to show a more aggressive look. The rear spoiler and front bumper displayed the word Shelby in block letters.

In mid-April of the 1968 production year, Ford introduced the GT 500KR and the 428 Cobra Jet engine. Equipped with reinforced shock towers, staggered rear shocks, and upgraded engine components, the GT 500KR was built for speed. The KR designation stood for "King of the Road." Rumor has it that Ford swiped the name from General Motors.

All KRs used a Ram Air induction system. The fiberglass chamber attached to the underside of the hood and funneled outside air directly to the air cleaner. The blue air cleaner cover replaced the Cobra oval air cleaner found on other Shelby models.

Only 1,251 GT 500KRs were produced. The production of the convertible version was even more limited–only 318 were produced.

A limited number of GT 500s were equipped with the 427 Low Riser engine and an automatic transmission. This engine featured forged steel crankshaft and rods, forged aluminum pistons, and mechanical lifters. The dual quad intake manifold used two Holley carburetors. Look for the "W" on the VIN to verify the original factory installed 427. These GT 500s are fast and rare.

While Shelby wanted to maintain the racing link with his street cars, by 1967 the GT 350 and GT 500 were morphing into Grand Touring vehicles.

Inspired by race cars, the pop-open gas cap was used throughout the Shelby Mustang production. Shelby used the GT 500 moniker because it was a bigger number than anyone else's.

Shelby vehicles used genuine wooden steering wheels and secondary gauges in the lower center console to impart a sports car look and feel to his Mustang derivatives.

It cost $4,472.57 to park the 1968 Shelby GT 500KR in your garage. Unlike years prior, the 1968 Shelby was adept in a straight line, but the heavy engine caused handling to suffer.

A roll bar was fitted to the 1968 GT 500KR for safety and to stiffen the chassis. Losing the top to make a convertible resulted in considerable cowl shake.

Essentially a Shelby version of the Cobra Jet Mustang, the 1968 GT 500KR was under-rated at 335 horsepower. It could cover the quarter-mile in the mid-14-second range.

1968 Mustangs

Overall, the 1968 Mustang line received minor cosmetic changes. The horizontal grille bars and the simulated side scoops were removed for a cleaner look. The "F-O-R-D" letters were removed from the hood, and the Mustang badge on the front fenders used script lettering instead of block letters.

The real changes took place under the hood. The familiar 289 V-8 was replaced with the new 302 V-8. The 302 would remain in the Mustang engine list for more than 20 years. Rated at 390 horsepower, the 427 V-8 was a popular engine option. Mustangs equipped with the 427 engine could reach 60 miles per hour in six seconds. The 427 V-8 was installed in 2,854 units and was only available with an automatic transmission.

The Sports Trim Group came with a woodgrain dash, knitted vinyl bucket seat inserts on hardtops and fastbacks, wheel well moldings, two-toned louvered hood, and styled steel wheels.

1968 GT

The GT Equipment Group was upgraded from the previous year. New 14-inch steel wheels were available in chrome or argent. Other changes included new graphics, GT emblems, and a pop-open fuel cap. The GT letters on the cap were changed from black to red. Louvers were installed on the C-pillars to bring fresh air into the back seat. Models equipped with an automatic transmission did not receive the GTA badge used in 1967.

A regional Mustang release was the High Country Special version. Sold in the Colorado area,
it used the same styling bits as the regional California Special, but had unique badging.

To raise the public profile of the Mustang, Ford introduced the California Special in 1968, a regional limited-production run that used some styling cues from the Shelby GT 350 to inject some visual excitement. Note the removal of the "Pony in the Corral" from the grille.

1968
Cobra Jet

On April 1, 1968, Ford introduced the 428 Cobra Jet engine as an option on the fastback and hardtop Mustangs. Performance fans were excited.

The Cobra Jet was an incredible engine. The front suspension shock towers were reinforced. A Ram Air induction setup and upgraded rear suspension shock absorbers were used on the four-speed models. Transmission options for the 428 Cobra Jet included a four-speed manual or six-speed automatic.

A wide black stripe covered the hood scoop and cowl and the GT Equipment Group was standard. To transfer the engine's power to the street, Cobra Jets came with Goodyear Polyglas F70x14 tires mounted on GT styled steel wheels. They were the best street tires available at the time.

Ford produced the Cobra Jet in limited numbers; 2,253 fastbacks and 564 hardtops. All are highly sought after by collectors.

Ford installed the rear spoiler and sequential taillights from the Shelby GT 350 Mustang. The added visual verve to the California Special. Unlike a Shelby, the side scoops on the California Special were for show only.

All California Specials were hardtop models in an effort to hold down costs. Approximately 5,000 were sold in 1968.

After the initial production run of 50 units, the 1968 Mustang Cobra Jet was available in any Mustang color, but a hood scoop was mandatory. It was essentially a street car stuffed with a racing engine and would bite the careless, hard.

Late in the 1968 Shelby production run, the GT 500KR was introduced. Packing a 428-ci Cobra Jet engine, it was loaded with every option possible.

The KR on the rocker panel of the 1968 GT 500KR stood for "King of the Road." Rumor has it that Shelby filched it from General Motors.

Right: Ford reaped incalculable publicity from the release of the 1968 Steve McQueen film *Bullitt*. The highlight of the movie was a vehicle chase through San Francisco with a 1968 Mustang GT fastback and a 1968 Dodge Hemi Charger R/T.

Left: Ford cleaned up the side scoop treatment and installed federally mandated side marker lights in 1968. Torq-Thrust wheels were a popular owner-installed upgrade.

In the latter half of 1968, Ford released the powerful 428-ci Cobra Jet engine in a run of 50 consecutive VIN Mustangs. They were painted white and went to friends of Ford that actively campaigned on the quarter-mile drag strips.

Mustang Sally

In 1966, singer Wilson Pickett recorded "Mustang Sally," a song about a woman who was in love with her 1965 Mustang. On November 26, 1966, the song entered the charts, rose to number 23 on the Top 40 list, and stayed on the list for nine weeks. The song remains a favorite of Mustang owners and music fans everywhere.

Playboy Bunnies Love Mustangs

Ford was selected as the Official Car of the Playboy's Playmate of the Year competition in 1964 and 1969. The first year, Donna Michelle received a 1964-1/2 convertible. Five years later, Connie Kreski received a Shelby GT 500. In 1967, Ford offered an exterior paint option called Playboy Pink.

Sonny and Cher were at the peak of popularity when the Mustang was introduced. They purchased custom-made his-and-hers models, and then produced the Sonny and Cher customizing car kit, which was only offered in 1966.

In 1966, Post cereals included Mustangs in their cereal boxes. The F&F Mold and Die Works in Dayton, Ohio, produced three-inch-long coupe, convertible, and 2+2 versions. Kids ripped open their cereal boxes to collect yellow, blue, green, and red Mustangs.

In 1999, Parker Brothers introduced a Mustang version of the popular Monopoly game. Players competed in buying, renting, and selling Mustangs. The traditional Monopoly game pewter pieces were replaced with a gasoline pump, 1999 coupe, 1965 steering wheel, styled steel wheel and tire, 1964-1/2 convertible, and 1965 front grille.

Mustang Toys

The Mustang was a true American success story. Ford sold one million pony cars in just two years. For those who couldn't afford to buy a GT, Shelby, or Mach 1, every popular Mustang model was quickly followed by a replica. In four decades, companies have offered Mustang enthusiasts thousands of model cars to build, toys to buy, and memorabilia to collect.

Dealer Promotions

AMF, the company that produced metal pedal cars, also offered a 1/12th scale miniature Ford that the dealers used in promotions. More than 16 inches long, these were the largest models available at the time.

Monogram struck a chord with modelers and racing fans with this version of the 1979 Mustang Indy pace car. Bill Coulter

The body was hinged at the front and opened to reveal a stamped metal chassis. A battery-powered motor powered the rear wheels. The headlights, taillights, and instrument panel lit up. The car moved forward, reverse, or could be set to run in a circle. It sold for $5.95 in 1967.

Hot Wheels

Mattel introduced the Hot Wheels diecast cars in 1968. The original line of Hot Wheels included the Custom Mustang that came in 16 color variations. Hot Wheels built their cars with Delrin axles to make them roll faster than other diecast cars on the market. In 1979 Mattel offered a Mustang Cobra in that year's line.

Model Car kits

Three different hobby kit manufacturers produced unassembled 1/32nd scale plastic models of the first generation of Mustangs using the 2+2 body style as the standard. AMF, Revell, and Monogram sold kits of the most important Mustangs for the next 40 years.

Revell-Monogram sold a 1965 Mustang in 1/24th scale. The model came packaged in a rare, collectible tin box. Revell-Monogram also produced plastic model kits of all three Mustang Indianapolis 500 Pace cars.

Shelby cars were popular with model makers. Even the Hertz 1966 GT 350H rental car was available in model form. Every Shelby model was reproduced in different scale sizes. AMT created model kits for the Shelby Cobra GT 500 and the Shelby Drag Team.

In the late 1970s, AMT and MPC both produced 1/25 scale models of the Mustang II hatchbacks. In 1982 Corgi of England produced a 1/43rd scale diecast replica of the Mustang hatchback. The hood and rear hatch opened to show off the engine details and interior.

Mustang in the Movies

According to the enthusiast website Mustang 123 (www.mustang123.com), Mustangs have been seen in over 350 movies since 1964. The list includes three James Bond films, several Oscar winning films, and a lot of straight to video specials. The most popular model seems to be the 1966 Mustang convertible.

The first movie Mustang appeared in was the film *Goldfinger*. James Bond, behind the wheel of an Aston Martin, chased the villain who drove a yellow 1965 convertible.

Below is a selected list of movies that have featured Mustangs.

Movie	Model	Movie	Model
52 Pickup	1969 fastback	Independence Day	1965 convertible
Alice's Restaurant	1965 convertible	Interview with a Vampire	1965 and 1966 convertibles
Apollo 13	1966 Shelby GT 350	JFK	1965 convertible
Beverly Hills Cop III	1966 convertible	Kiss the Girls	1966 coupe
Bull Durham	1968 Shelby Convertible GT 350	The Love Bug	1966 coupe
Bullitt	1968 fastback	Love Story	1966 Shelby Fastback GT 350H
The Candidate	1966 coupe	Omega Man	1970 convertible
Cape Fear (1991)	1965 convertible	The Pelican Brief	1966 coupe
Casino	1966 convertible	Play Misty for Me	1966 convertible
Dazed and Confused	1965 convertible	Predator II	1966 coupe
Diamonds Are Forever	1971 Mach 1	The Rookie	1965 coupe
The Doors	1966 convertible	Star Trek IV	1968 coupe
Dragnet	1966 convertible	Summer of Sam	1965 convertible
The French Connection	1965 coupe	The Thomas Crown Affair	1968 Shelby GT 500 convertible
Goldfinger	1965 convertible	Thunderball	1965 convertible
Gone in 60 Seconds	1973 Mach 1	Up Close and Personal	1966 convertible
Gone in 60 Seconds (2000)	1967 Shelby GT 350	Who Is Harry Crumb?	1966 convertible

These are diecast models of the three Mustang Indy pace cars. Clockwise: Brooklin 1/43rd scale 1964 Mustang Indy pace car, Jouef 1/18th scale 1994 Mustang Indy pace car, and a Johnny Lightning 1/64th 1979 Mustang Indy pace car. Bill Coulter

1969

Mustangs were significantly restyled in 1969. The fastback was renamed the SportsRoof, and all performance models received the body modifications. Forty-four percent of all Mustangs sold this year were fastbacks.

Modifications included lowering the body 0.5 inches on the suspension and increasing the windshield rake by 2.2 degrees. The roofline was lowered by 0.9 inches.

The front grille was enlarged and featured four round headlights for the first time. Simulated side scoops and a rear spoiler were added high on the rear fenders of the fastback models.

The Deluxe Interior Décor Group carried the performance image to the inside of the car. The Mach 1, Boss 429, and Grande models featured simulated woodgrain appliques on the doors, console, and instrument panel.

Continuing the tradition of triple-element taillights, the 1969 Mustang fitted the lenses in a concave panel. Base price for a convertible was $2,832.

The GT model put in a limited appearance in 1969, when it was found to be competiton against the Mach 1. Thus, the GT was quietly shown off of the stage.

Quad headlights were fitted to all 1969 Mustangs, while race-inspired hood hold-down pins were standard with the performance-orientated Mach 1 model.

In order to compete in the SCCA's Trans-Am racing series, Ford had to build at least 1,000 street versions of the 1969 Boss 302. When the dust settled, 1,628 units were constructed.

Larry Shinoda designed the attention-grabbing graphic tape package on the 1969 Boss 302.
He also insisted that the phony rear quarter-panel scoops be smoothed out.

Except for the massive functional hood scoop and the small script on the front fender, one might mistake the 1969 Boss 429 for a grocery getter. A very fast grocery getter.

1969
The Mustang Grande

The Grande was a luxury model designed to compete with the Mercury Cougar and upscale versions of the Camaro and Firebird.

On the outside, the Grande featured wire wheel covers, dual color-keyed mirrors, a two-toned paint stripe, wheelwell rocker panels, rear deck moldings, and Grande script lettering on the C-pillars.

The biggest difference in the Deluxe Décor Group was the added insulation. Increasing 50 pounds to the weight of the car, heavy sound-deadening pads were installed under the carpets. The Grande package could be ordered with any engine option.

Built to satisfy NASCAR's requirement that a race engine be production based, the 1969 Boss 429 was strangled on the street by the use of a restrictive carburetor and exhaust system. Replacing them with larger components unleashed a torrent of power.

A beast in sleeper's clothes, the 1969 Boss 429 was only available in the SportsRoof body style. Most lead hard lives and rack up miles a quarter-mile at a time.

The 1969 Mach 1

The Mach 1 replaced the GT as the Mustang performance leader. Everything about this car said speed and performance. Spoilers, stripes, and scoops told the street that the Mach 1 was ready to fly. Optional NASCAR-inspired hood latches reinforced the racer image. The hood was painted flat black and came with a simulated hood scoop similar to the 1968-1/2 Cobra Jet.

Side and tail stripes coordinated with the body color. Body-colored racing mirrors were an industry first. The chromed pop-open gas cap and wheels finished off the exterior styling.

The Competition Suspension package featured heavier springs and shocks and a larger front sway bar. The four-speed Mach 1 came with staggered rear shocks. Goodyear Polyglas GT tires with raised white lettering were standard equipment on the Mach 1.

The Mach 1's Deluxe Interior Group featured Rim-Blow steering wheel, console, high-back bucket seats, and the special insulation option installed on the luxury Grande model.

The 351 two-barrel V-8 was the Mach 1's standard engine. The 428 Cobra Jet Ram Air engine was the most sought after option. The 390-ci V-8 was also available. The Mach 1 could cover a quarter-mile in less than 14 seconds.

Ford built 72,450 Mach 1 models in 1969.

The Boss Arrives

Ford knew performance enthusiasts wanted a car that could combine raw acceleration with great handling. Ford needed a car that could face the competition in the Sports Car Club of America (SCCA) racing circuit requiring at least 1,000 cars be sold to the public to qualify as a racing model. The Boss 302 arrived ready to run.

The Boss 302 was based on the SportsRoof body without the side body scoops. The hood, rear deck, taillight panel, and grille area where the headlights were mounted were all painted black. A front spoiler kept the nose low to the ground at high speeds.

Boss options included an adjustable rear wing and rear window slats. Distinctive wheels set off the exterior design. Argent-painted Magnum 500 wheels carried large F60x15 Goodyear Polyglas tires. The suspension and shock towers were reinforced to handle the stresses of high-speed cornering.

The only engine option was the Boss 302, which was matched with a four-speed manual transmission. This Mustang could go from 0 to 60 in under seven seconds and cover a quarter-mile in under 15 seconds. For reliability, the 302 engine was a rev-limiter that protected the engine from racing over 6,150 rpm.

The standard equipment list included front disc brakes, quick ratio steering, staggered rear shocks, and color-keyed rearview mirrors.

A large stripe along the side featured Boss 302 lettering. Exterior colors were Wimbledon White, Bright Yellow, Calypso Coral, and Acapulco Blue.

The Boss 429

Like the 302, the 429 was inspired by professional racing standards. This time around, it was NASCAR. Ford shipped 500 SportsRoof models to custom builder Kar Kraft for modifications and final assembly in order to qualify. Spring towers were repositioned to allow the massive engine and transmission to fit.

On the outside, the 429 kept the simulated side scoops and front spoiler found on other SportsRoof models. Other small visual clues included the fender decals and large hood scoop.

Standard Boss 429 equipment included an engine oil cooler, trunk-mounted battery, power disc brakes, power steering, close ratio four-speed transmission, staggered rear shocks, manual choke, and an operational hood scoop. The springs found on the 429 were the heavier than any other Mustang model, and it was the first Mustang to have a rear sway bar installed.

The exterior colors that were offered with Boss 429 were Raven Black, Black Jade, Royal Maroon, Candy Apple Red, Wimbledon White, and Blue.

Inboard the F60x15 Polyglas tires were manual front disc brakes. They are handy when the engine puts out at least 410 foot-pounds of torque at 3,400 rpm.

Nothing fancy here, just standard Mustang interior. The Boss 429 buyer knew that the extra $1,208 spent went under the hood, not in the cabin.

Because the Boss 429 required such extensive modifications to build, Ford had Kar Kraft assemble the finished product. The identification plate on the driver's door designated the vehicle as NASCAR-approved.

Intended as the finest handling Ford built, the 1969 Boss 302 didn't disappoint. This example, set-up for road course racing, shows the aggressive appearance and stance that set the Boss apart.

With the famed Shaker Hood Scoop poking through the hood of the 1969 Mach 1, the 428-ci Cobra Jet engine was a potent contender at stoplight drag races. It could cover the quarter-mile in the low-14s.

Tremendous front overhang was susceptible to damage if the driver had depth-perception issues. Factory fog lamps were mounted under the bumper and wore protective covers until needed.

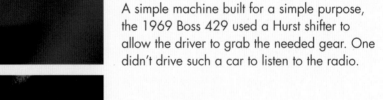

A simple machine built for a simple purpose, the 1969 Boss 429 used a Hurst shifter to allow the driver to grab the needed gear. One didn't drive such a car to listen to the radio.

A conservative speedometer was standard on the 1969 Boss 302. The lack of a redline on the tachometer was indicative of the engine's propensity to spin. A rev-limiter protected the engine.

The American Muscle Car

In the 1960s, street performance was measured in quarter-mile increments. Every car manufacturer brought out its own version of street racer. By the late 1960s, engines were getting larger and more powerful, and the car bodies were growing to fit the high horsepower powerplants. Names like Challenger, Barracuda, Road Runner, Cougar, Corvette, Charger, and GTO inspired many late-night boulevard runs.

By 1971, the muscle car era was on its way out. Rising insurance premiums made high performance cars expensive to drive. Car buyers were becoming more interested in comfort and quality instead of horsepower and 0 to 60 numbers.

1966 Chevrolet Corvair Monza

The sporty little Corvair was offered in two-door, four-door, coupe, and convertible models. The base model was powered by air-cooled horizontal six-cylinder engine. A turbocharged option delivered 180 horsepower. The European-inspired interior came with bucket seats and a telescopic steering wheel. Ralph Nader's book, *Unsafe at Any Speed*, helped put the Corvair in the history books thanks to its poor safety rating.

1964 Plymouth Barracuda

The Barracuda was Plymouth's first response to the Mustang. Based on the Valiant body, the most dramatic feature of the Barracuda was the huge opening rear window. Developed by Pittsburgh Plate Glass Company, it was the largest piece of glass found on any car.

Three engine options were offered. Two were based on Chrysler's inline six cylinder and the other was a 273-ci, 180 horsepower V-8. Advertising for the Barracuda called attention to "the nifty new fastback that seats five and costs less than $2,500." Unfortunately sales didn't catch on.

1968 American Motors AMX 390

The name AMX is short for American Motors Experimental. The AMX was the first steel-bodied, two-seat American production car since the 1957 Ford Thunderbird.

Introduced as the 1968-1/2 model at the Chicago Auto Show in February 1968, the AMX was powered by a 315 horsepower, 390-ci V-8 that launched the car from 0 to 60 in 6.6 seconds. It was base priced at $3,245, and the AMX unfortunately didn't survive to its third year of production.

In February 1968, race car driver Craig Breedlove set speed records with an AMX. A limited number of red-white-and-blue Craig Breedlove models were built to commemorate the record-setting event.

1967 Chevrolet Camaro SS

On September 29, 1966, Chevrolet introduced its answer to the Mustang. The Camaro was offered with a range of engine options. The small-block RPO L48 350-ci V-8 delivered 295 horsepower was popular with performance enthusiasts. The SS 350 package included special badges, wide tires, upgraded suspension components, louvered hood, and fat stripe around the nose.

In November 1966, Chevrolet introduced two 396 big-block V-8 engine options. The 396 covered the quarter-mile in 14.5 seconds, and went from 0 to 60 in six seconds.

1970 Dodge Challenger T/A

Chrysler Corporation's Dodge division built the Challenger T/A to compete in the Sports Car Club of America's (SCCA) TransAmerican Sedan Championship series.

The flat back hood on the Challenger T/A was equipped with a functional hood scoop and lock pins to hold it down. At the other end of the car, an increased rear spring camber lifted the rear high enough to accommodate wide tires and dual exhaust.

Wide decals lined the side of the Challenger to let other drivers know this one was ready to run. The T/A covered the quarter-mile in 14.5 seconds.

1968 Plymouth Road Runner

Plymouth introduced the Road Runner in 1968 to meet car enthusiasts demand for an affordable performance car. Using Warner Brothers' cartoon character as its namesake, the Road Runner's horn imitated the popular "beep-beep" heard every Saturday morning.

The $2,870 two-door sedan came with a 335 horsepower, 383-ci V-8 engine. A four-speed transmission, heavy-duty suspension, 11-inch drum brakes, and Red Stripe tires were standard equipment.

1969 Pontiac GTO "The Judge"

The Judge was released on December 19, 1968. It was originally available in bright orange with tri-color stripes, and other GTO colors were eventually added as options. The special edition GTO came with a blacked-out grille, Rally II wheels, functional hood scoops, and Judge decals on the front fenders. A 60-inch rear deck airfoil was found on the car this year.

Standard engine was the 400-ci, 366 horsepower Ram Air III V-8 mated with a three-speed transmission. The Judge package was offered in hardtop or convertible body styles. The wild Judge raced through the quarter-mile in 14.45 seconds.

1969–1970
The Last Shelby Mustangs

In 1969 the GT 350 and GT 500 models were offered in fastback and convertible versions. The fastback model used the Mustang Mach 1 body as its base platform.

The last Shelby Mustang came off the production line in 1969. At the end of year, 789 cars were carried forward and renamed 1970 models. The cars were updated by changing the VIN number and adding twin black hood stripes and a Boss 302 chin spoiler.

In the final version, the front end styling was different from previous models. Lucas fog lamps were mounted beneath the chrome steel bumper.

Scoops were everywhere. The fiberglass hood featured three forward facing NACA scoops and two rear facing scoops. The fenders had scoops to cool the front and rear brakes. On the convertible models, the rear scoop was mounted lower to not interfere with the convertible mechanism.

Only 194 Shelby GT 350 convertibles were built in 1969. Prices started at $4,753; almost $2,000 more than a standard Mustang convertible.

ABOVE: The three-part rear spoiler, hood, and front fenders were constructed of fiberglass. Taillights from the 1965 Thunderbird were fitted for dramatic impact.

Three NACA ducts and two vents were built into the 1969 Shelby hood. The front two let air into the engine compartment, while the other pair let the air out. The center duct fed outside air into the air cleaner.

LEFT: When Ford bulked-up the 1969 Mustang, the Shelby had to follow suit. The stretched nose required special fiberglass front fenders, hood, and grille. Silver Jade, paint code 4, was one of 11 colors available.

While not designed for drag strip duty, the 1969 Shelby GT 350 acquitted itself with a 0 to 60–miles per hour time in the low 7-second range. The tape stripe running the length was made of reflective material.

This is the standard wheel cover for the 1968 Shelby Mustang. Most buyers sprang for the optional alloy wheels, and many vehicles that used wheelcovers when new have since been fitted with the optional wheels.

Shelby had some 1969 GT 350s and GT 500s left at the end of the year, so twin black stripes were painted on the hood and the FBI was called in to supervise the fitting of 1970 VIN to allow Shelby to sell the remaining vehicles as 1970 models.

The small front scoops on the 1969–1970 Shelby GT 350 were designed to direct cooling air to the 11.3-inch front disc brakes. In a vehicle weighing over 3,200 pounds, effective brakes were highly desired.

Mustang in the 1970s

The front grille received minor design refinements this year. Dual headlights returned and were mounted inside the grille opening. At the rear, the taillights were recessed in a flat panel, and the simulated side scoops were removed to resemble the cleaner look of the Boss 302.

The Mach 1 was equipped with color-keyed racing mirrors, competition suspension, and sport wheel covers. The hood was updated with twist latches instead of the NASCAR pins used on the 1969 version. The flat black paint used on the hood in previous years was replaced with a wide stripe. Large Mach 1 lettering updated the graphics package. For racing, the Drag Pack option was offered with the 428 CJ Ram Air engine, shaker scoop, engine oil cooler, and beefed-up connecting rods.

The 1970 Boss 429 remained essentially unchanged from 1969. Production declined to less than 500 units. The fastback Boss was developed as a stock car racing platform and featured a 302 V-8 rated at 290 horsepower.

Only 96 Twister models were made in 1970, making them one of the rarest Mustangs. The rear spoiler was adjustable for angle of attack.

Left: Built as a regional model for Kansas, the 1970 Twister was intended to be a 428-ci Cobra Jet Mustang with orange paint and special graphics. When sufficient big-block engines couldn't be secured, 351-ci Cleveland engines were installed.

Left: Built for just this kind of treatment, the 1970 Boss 302 was arguably the finest handling four-seat street machine available. A beefy front sway bar, as well as a rear bar, helped minimize body roll under hard cornering.

The top engine in the 1970 Mach 1 was the 428-ci Super Cobra Jet. Built for drag-strip use, the powerplant was stuffed full of top-shelf speed equipment such as a special crankshaft, 427 Le Mans–type connecting rods, and an oil cooler.

Call-out numbers that denote the engine displacement in cubic inches flank the non-functional hood scoop on this 1970 Mach 1. Strong graphics and sparkling performance were demanded by buyers to make points each Saturday night.

Left: Rear window Sport Slats were a $65 option, and the rear spoiler went for $20 and was only available on SportsRoof models.

The rear shock absorbers on the 1970 Mach 1 with the Competiton Suspension and the 428 Cobra Jet–equipped Mach 1s were staggered to minimize rear axle hop under heavy acceleration.

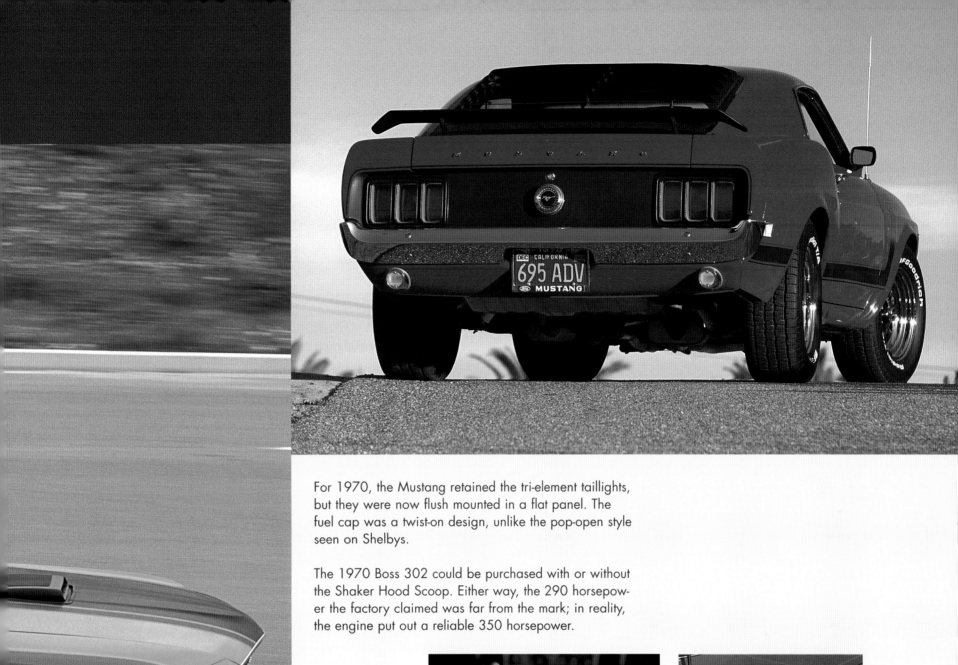

For 1970, the Mustang retained the tri-element taillights, but they were now flush mounted in a flat panel. The fuel cap was a twist-on design, unlike the pop-open style seen on Shelbys.

The 1970 Boss 302 could be purchased with or without the Shaker Hood Scoop. Either way, the 290 horsepower the factory claimed was far from the mark; in reality, the engine put out a reliable 350 horsepower.

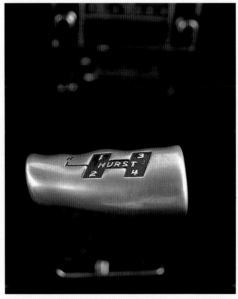

Ford installed a beefy Hurst shifter in the 1970 Boss 302 to minimize mis-shifts under heavy loads. Retail price on the near-track ready car was $3,720.

When struck by headlights or if the sun hit the 1970 Boss 302's reflective tape in the right way, the graphics glowed. This was as much a safety item as a stylistic point.

1971 | The 1971 Mustangs were the largest and heaviest models to date. Ford engineers stretched the wheelbase to 109 inches, and the weight increased by 200 pounds. The 1971 models represented the final revisions of the original Mustang body before the Mustang II arrived in 1974.

The Mustang was offered in three configurations: hardtop, convertible, and SportsRoof. The angle on the rear window of the SportsRoof model was only 14 inches from being horizontal, which made it hard to see out of. For the first time, the SportsRoof could be ordered with an optional vinyl roof.

Mach 1 SportsRoof fastback hardtop was the Mustang performance king. Muscle car performance was on its way out because of stringent federal emissions standards, but the 1971 Mach 1 was still a worthy street competitor. Equipped with a 429 Cobra Jet V-8 engine and automatic transmission, the Mach 1 could reach 60 miles per hour in 8.1 seconds.

This Mustang Boss line ended in 1971. The Boss 351 started with Mach 1 standard equipment and added functional hood scoops, Boss 351 body decals, chrome front bumper, and front spoiler. The front and rear valance panels, rocker panels, and hood were painted black or argent silver to contrast with the body color. Approximately 1,800 models were priced at $4,124—a $1,000 more than the Mach 1.

Classic pony car proportions were carried to extremes with the release of the 1971 Mach 1. Ford decreed that the Mustang would be able to handle any size engine in the Ford catalog, hence an enormous engine compartment.

The last year for the Boss series was 1971, when the Boss 351 debuted. Under the hood was a potent 351-ci Cleveland V-8 that generated 330 horsepower.

In order to fit large engines under the hood, the 1971 Mach 1 increased in width to 74.1 inches. The weight increased and tipped the scales at 3,560 pounds.

With a rear window only 14 degrees from horizontal, the 1971 Mustang Mach 1 sacrificed rear seat head room for an aggressive profile. A Kamm-inspired rear end aided in aerodynamics and reduced drag.

The Mustang first turned a wheel on a race track when it was still a concept car. Unveiled at the U.S. Grand Prix at Watkins Glen in October 1962, Dan Gurney drove pace laps in the white-and-blue tubular-framed sports car. Two weeks later, at the Pacific Grand Prix at California's Laguna Seca race course, the crowd reacted with excited cheers. What did Ford have in mind for the future? The sleek fiberglass Mustang I is now on display at the Henry Ford Museum in Dearborn, Michigan.

Officially, Ford Motor Company was out of the racing business. When Lee Iacocca replaced Bob McNamara, one of his first objectives was to revive the motorsports racing program. To get started, Ford shipped four notchback Mustangs to Europe to participate in the 1964 Monte Carlo Rally and Tour de France circuit.

The cars were early production models upgraded and modified to handle the punishment of endurance racing. Mustang won its share of races and spread the word that American horsepower was ready to compete.

Mustangs participated in a limited number of European racing events until 1970, but after 1964, Ford management turned its attention homeward.

Shelby GT 350R Racing

Ford teamed with legendary race car driver Carroll Shelby to create a line of high performance Mustangs. Built for the track as well as the street, the distinctive white and blue striped Shelby cars are true American legends.

Production Mustang fastbacks were shipped from Ford's San Jose assembly plant to Shelby's operation near the Los Angeles International Airport. Ford wanted Shelby to turn the Mustang into a high-performance model. Racing history says he successfully met that objective. To qualify under Sports Car Club of America (SCCA) sanctioning rules, Shelby built the first 100 GT 350s in a short period of time.

Thirty-seven cars were heavily modified with racing parts and components. The engine, chassis, suspension, bodywork, and interiors were completely reworked with racing performance in mind. The stock Hi-Po 289 V-8 engine was rated at 271 horsepower. After Shelby's modifications, the horsepower rating exceeded 450 horsepower.

The GT 350R models were true racing cars. The first of domestic racing victories came at a Sports Car Club of America B/Production event on Valentine's Day 1965 in Green Valley, Texas. Shelby Mustangs won the SCCA national titles in 1965 and 1966. Many of the original 37 GT 350R models can still be found racing in vintage car events.

Mustang at the Drag Strip

In 1965, Mustangs found their way to drag strips. Bob Tasca of Tasca Ford in East Providence, Rhode Island, was the first to enter officially sanctioned drag competitions. Tasca entered his modified Mustangs in the A/FX (factory experimental class).

Based on those early successes, Ford built ten A/FX drag racing Mustangs. Some models were equipped with 427 High Riser engines, but the real drag king was the 427 Cammer. The engine featured special head castings and single overhead camshafts and delivered 650 horsepower to the track. Both engines accelerated the customized Mustangs to the finish line in just over 10 seconds at over 125 miles per hour. With more modifications for the Top Fuel class, the horsepower rating rose to almost 2,000.

Trans-Am Racing

Ford and Shelby did not field a factory sponsored GT 350R racing team after the 1965. Instead Ford entered SCCA's new Trans-American Sedan racing series. Shelby assisted in the development of the Group II Mustangs. The Trans-Am series was created to promote production models instead of exotic racing machines.

The first Trans-Am race was held at Sebring, Florida, in March 1966. Ford participated in the SCCA Trans-Am series until the end of the decade. For many race fans and automotive reporters, 1970 is considered the best year in the series. Every major automobile manufacturer sponsored a racing team. Starting grids included cars from Chevrolet, Ford, Pontiac, American Motors, Plymouth, and Dodge.

The 1970 Mustang Boss 302 represented the high point in Ford racing. Using a factory body and the best suspension and engine components available, the Boss 302 was hard to beat. Ford ended the year as Trans-Am champion. One month after the victory, Ford ceased all motorsports racing activities.

The Return to Racing

The Mustang's return to racing was inspired by an engineer at Ford of Germany. Based on the Fox chassis Mustang, Eric Zakspeed built a race car to compete in the International Motor Sports Association (IMSA) series.

The IMSA Mustang cars were powered by a turbocharged 1.7 liter, four-cylinder engine that delivered an amazing 700 horsepower. While earlier Mustang race cars closely resembled the stock models sold at the same time, the IMSA cars were barely recognizable as true Mustangs. Jack Roush organized his own IMSA Mustang race team and dominated the series for many years.

Ford and Roush also returned to SCCA Trans-Am racing. In 1989, the Mustang finished first in the SCCA standings for the first time since 1970. In the 1994 Trans-Am season, the Roush Racing Team became the first team in history with 50 wins. Tom Kendall drove a Mustang in the record-setting win.

The Saleen/Allen Speed Lab Team won the SCCA World Challenge Manufacturer's Championship in 1996. Television and movie star Tim Allen was part owner.

Winning at the racetrack has always had an impact on sales at the local dealership. The Mustang's long history of racing victories did its part to sell millions of cars to drivers who did their racing during the commute to work every day.

There isn't much of a difference between the 1971 and 1972 model years. Ford engineers spent their time working on the development of the next generation Mustang. The quickest way to tell the difference in model years was to look at the Mustang signature on the back of the car. The Mustang lettering was changed from block letters to script in 1972.

The new federal emissions standards kept the engineers busy. The Mustang's engine list was reduced to five options. The Boss 351 and big-block 429 engines were dropped from the options list.

The Mustang model offerings expanded to offer every kind of driver a choice. Five two-door body styles, two hardtops, two SportsRoofs (fastbacks), and a convertible were offered.

The 1972 Mach 1 SportsRoof fastback hardtop came with a series of upgrades from the base Mustang including hood scoops, competition suspension, front spoiler bumper, color-keyed hood and rear fender moldings, wheel trim rings, and whitewall tires. The standard engine was the 302-ci, two-barrel carbureted V-8.

By 1973, the Mach 1 has fell victim to a performance decline due to increasing emission regulations. Technology could provide strong performance or low emissions, just not at the same time.

The Sprint A new exterior trim package was added mid-year. The Sprint, named to commemorate the 1972 Olympics, had a large "U.S.A." emblem added to passenger side right rear fender. The Sprint package was available on hardtop and fastback models and were painted white with red and blue stripes on the hood, rear panel, and lower body panels. The Sprint package was purely cosmetic, and there were no special engine or handling modifications included. A limited edition of 50 Sprint convertibles were built for a Cherry Day Parade in Washington, D.C. There were a total of 800 Sprint models produced.

Ford tried to certify their four-barrel V-8 for use in the 1973 Mach 1 by submitting data from a two-barrel engine. The government caught the ruse and forced the Mach 1 to use the smaller carburetor. The stronger engine ended up in 266 horsepower Q-code Mustangs such as this yellow example.

1973 Mustang

The era of the big Mustang came to an end in 1973. The word on the street was Ford planned to introduce a new model next year. The anticipation for what was coming hung over the 1973 model lineup.

The 1973 Mustangs were almost identical to the 1972 versions. All 1973 Mustangs featured new color-keyed molded front bumpers to meet the federal government's crash test mandate. A new grille used vertical turn-signals.

Influenced by new federal safety regulations that convertibles would no longer be offered after the 1973 model year, the Mustang didn't offer a ragtop for the next 10 years.

The 1973 Mach 1 received a new stripe treatment. A new vinyl roof option was available on the Mach 1 as well as the other SportsRoof models. The standard hood featured nonfunctioning hood scoops. The scoops worked when the Mach 1 was equipped with the 351 engine option. The Mach 1 hood could be ordered with a Tu-Tone paint treatment. The customized hood was painted flat black or silver and featured twist-type hood locks.

When the 1973 Mach 1 hit the streets, word was out that it was the last year of the large cruiser. Sales for the model rose to 35,440, up from 27,675 units the prior year.

Convertible Mustangs bid adieu in 1973 and stepped away from the market for a number of years. Forged aluminum wheels that debuted in 1973 had a flaw that forced Ford to recall them.

Ford designers came up with a stylish solution to incorporate the federally mandated front 5-miles-per-hour bumpers to the Mustang in 1973. The rear bumper mounted away from the body to comply with the 2-1/2-miles-per-hour impact requirement.

Top: A center console was a $53.40 option on the Grande model, but it was $67.95 on all others. Highback seats were carried over from prior years.

Ginger was what Ford called this 1973 Mustang interior hue. SelectShift Cruise-O-Matic automatic transmission was a $203.73 option.

Right: A beefy Hurst shifter was used in the 1971 Boss 351. Center console option with clock retailed for $76 when installed in the Boss model.

In 1973, the Hardtop model used flowing C-pillars to suggest the lines of the SportsRoof version while retaining a conventional rear window. Trim rings and hubcaps went for $31.08 on non-Grande models.

Ever since its debut in April 1964, the Mustang had grown. By 1973, it was a hefty version of the lithe pony car envisioned by Lee Iacocca.

1974
Mustang Coupe

Rising insurance rates and the OPEC oil embargo turned car buyers away from gas-guzzling performance cars to smaller, more fuel efficient models. Downsizing was the word of the day.

The new Mustang II reflected those sensibilities. The new design was 7 inches shorter than the original 1964-1/2 model, and 13 inches shorter than the 1973 generation. Lee Iacocca asked his team of engineers and designers to create "a little jewel." Ghia, recently acquired by Ford, did some of the initial design work on the Mustang II. The new car incorporated styling elements from the original Mustang. The front grille and sculptured side panels were reminiscent of the first model.

The Mustang II was classified as a subcompact. Standard engine was a 2,300-cc inline four-cylinder engine. A front subframe isolated the engine from the rest of the chassis to

Lee Iacocca wanted the Mustang II to behave like a "little limousine." Ford's association with Italian design firm Ghia helped plush-up the diminutive four-seater.

RIGHT: Like Mustangs before it, the Mustang II retained the tri-element taillights that had been used since 1965. However, opera windows, vinyl half-roof, and simulated wire lace wheels were never seen on the original Mustang.

LEFT: Bold graphics and a V-8 fender emblem hinted at glory days past on the 1978 Mustang II Cobra II, a $724 package.

dampen vibration. Instead of competing with Camaros and Firebirds, the Mustang II was compared side by side to General Motors models like the Skyhawk and Starfire.

During the five years of production, the Mustang II body style did not change. Hardtop and fastback body styles were the only choices. Convertibles were not offered during the Mustang II 1974 to 1978 production years.

The Ghia model replaced the previous year's Grande. The Ghia Notchback came with color-keyed Deluxe seatbelts, dual color-keyed remote control door mirrors, Super Sound package, shag carpeting, wood-tone door panel accents, digital clock, vinyl or cloth interior, color-keyed vinyl roof, and spoke-style wheel covers.

Other overall improvements included rack and pinion steering, front disc brakes, staggered shock rear suspension, and a four-speed manual transmission.

1975
Mustang

Throughout its five-year life cycle, the Mustang II received minor changes from year to year. In 1975, the major changes included the addition of a V-8 engine and the moonroof options.

The Luxury Interior Group was standard on the Ghia model. The interior was upgraded with deluxe door and rear seat trim, courtesy lights, color-keyed seatbelts, shag carpeting, and a premium sound system. The final step was the Ghia Luxury Group, which included silver metallic paint, a half vinyl roof, and full-length pinstripes. The roofline was changed to incorporate an opera window. As a signal of luxury, a stand-up hood ornament was added. Inside, the interior was dressed in velour cloth on the console, headliner, and sun visor.

1976
Mustang Stallion

The Stallion appearance package could be ordered in the coupe or fastback models. Stallion design elements included black moldings and wiper arms, a black grille that did not carry the usual pony emblem, black rocker panels, lower fenders, lower doors, lower front and rear bumpers, and black lower quarter panels. The package included styled wheels and large stallion decals on the front fenders. This same exterior treatment was also offered on the Ford Maverick and Pinto.

1976-77
Cobra II

Ford introduced the Cobra II in 1976 to rekindle the performance image it enjoyed a decade earlier. Inspired by the dramatic striping on 1960s-era Shelby Mustangs, the Cobra II was completely decked out.

The Cobra II modification package included front air spoiler; rear deck lid spoiler; simulated hood scoop; quarter window louvers with snake emblems; and accent stripes on the front spoiler, hood, roof, rear deck, rear deck spoiler, and lower body panels. The snake emblem was also located on the fenders, wheels, and blacked-out grille.

The four-cylinder was standard and a V-6 and 302 V-8 were offered as options.

Available only as a fastback, the Cobra II was offered in three colors: white with blue stripes, blue with white stripes, and black with gold stripes. The last option was reminiscent of the GT 350ZH Hertz rent-a-racer.

In 1977, the Sports Performance Package added a four-speed manual transmission. When used with the 302, the combination helped the Cobra II live up to its performance image.

1977 Mustang

The 1977 model changes were limited to an expanded list of exterior colors and interior trim options. The Mustang II body style was never offered in a convertible version, but 1977 brought some relief to open air fans with the introduction of the new T-Top. Twin removable bronze-tinted glass panels were usually stored in the trunk. The T-Top option was only available on the three-door fastback models. The price for the feel of the wind in your hair was almost $600.

The SportsRoof appearance package was upgraded to include a sport steering wheel, styled steel wheels with raised white letters, and a brushed aluminum instrument panel.

The four-cylinder Mustang equipped with a four-speed transmission received a 26 miles per gallon city/highway rating from the EPA. Fuel economy be damned, the Sports Performance Package included a 302-ci V-8 engine, four-speed transmission, power steering and brakes, and 195/70R WSW tires.

The Appearance Décor Group included a Tu-Tone paint treatment on the lower body panels, thin pinstripes, styled wheels with trim rings, and upgraded cloth or vinyl interior options.

Luxury buyers could add the Ghia Sports Group. Black or tan paint, chamois or black half-vinyl roof, vinyl insert bodyside moldings, pinstripes, luggage rack with color-matched hold down straps, spoked aluminum wheels with chamois painted spokes, and blacked-out grille. In the interior, the Ghia seat trim was finished in chamois with black upper inserts. Ghia applique inserts on the instrument panel and leather-wrapped steering wheel dressed up the interior.

1978 Mustang King Cobra

The final year for the Mustang II body style was 1978. During 1974 to 1978, production of the Cobra edition was limited. The King Cobra, offered only in 1978, had the lowest build numbers.

The King Cobra package for the fastback model was the last cosmetic version of the Mustang II. A large snake decal covered the hood, which had a nonfunctioning scoop. A front airdam and rear wheel well spoilers contributed to the race-inspired design.

Standard features included the 302 V-8 engine, four-speed transmission, power brakes, power steering, aluminum wheels, and the Rallye handling package with heavy duty springs, adjustable shocks, and a rear sway bar. The T-top was optional.

A far cry from the performance days of 1970, the engine compartment of the 1978 Mustang II Cobra II housed a 302-ci V-8 with only 139 horsepower.

The blacked-out egg crate grille set off the chrome galloping pony on the 1978 Mustang II Ghia model. Lights in grille were actually turn-signals.

The Mustang II had little under the hood to entertain, so the task fell to an AM/FM stereo 8-track system.

Costing $69 more than the Boss 429 option, the 1978 Mustang II King Cobra package went for a staggering $1,277. The T-top option set a buyer back an additional $647.

Introducing the Third Generation

The Mustang II era was over. The next generation of Mustangs was introduced in 1979. The new Mustang, designed around the Fox platform, looked nothing like the original pony car. Reflecting a European design influence, the nose, grille, and raked windshield had a cleaner, more aerodynamic look and feel. Aerodynamics were becoming important in automotive design. The new Mustang's coefficient of drag (CD) was 25 percent less than the Mustang II.

Four engines were offered in 1979. The 2.3 liter, four-cylinder offered in the Mustang II was standard. The 2.8 liter V-6 was optional. For performance enthusiasts, Ford offered a turbocharged 2.3 liter, four-cylinder engine. The turbocharger was an attempt to combine the high mileage benefit of a small engine with the high performance of a V-8. Ford claimed the four-cylinder saved owners more than $500 in maintenance costs compared to other cars.

The popular 302 V-8 5.0 liter was the final engine option. The name was changed to the 5.0L to reflect the shift to metric measures.

The third generation Mustang was offered as two-door sedan and three-door hatchback.

The 1979 Mustang had exceptional handling. State-of-the-art Michelin TRX tires were offered as options. Mounted on specially designed rims and combined with handling performance pieces like sway bars, shocks, and springs, the Mustang lives up to the presentation.

Customers voted on the new Mustang design with their wallets. Sales of the 1979 Mustang ranked seventh that year.

1979 Cobra

The Cobra was only available in the fastback body style. The turbocharged four-cylinder engine was standard. Although the turbocharged engine received a lot of hype when it was introduced, mechanical problems plagued the powerplant. The engine was removed from the Mustang engine family after the 1980 model year.

From 1979 to 1981, the Cobra was the performance leader in the Mustang line. Other than the limited edition Indy pace car, the Cobra was the only other special model offered in 1979.

The new interior made the driver feel right at home. Speedometer, tachometer, fuel, temperature, oil pressure, and ammeter were placed in front of the driver. The Cobra featured a black dash treatment instead of the woodgrain pattern used on other models.

Ford had purchased the legal rights to use the Cobra name from Carroll Shelby, but had not bought the GT 350 name. Was anyone surprised when Shelby's lawyers took Ford to court?

The Indianapolis 500 is called the greatest spectacle in racing. Every spring, the best race drivers in the world come to the brickyard to compete. Each year, Indianapolis 500 officials select a pace car to lead the racers around the track. In the past 40 years, Mustangs have served as the Indianapolis 500 pace in 1964, 1979, and 1994.

The first time was six weeks after the Mustang was introduced. Ford engineers produced three 1964-1/2 convertibles for the race. One served as the official pace car, and the other two were available backups in case there was a mechanical problem. All three pace cars were equipped with special equipment including flag stanchions and grab handles—two beside the rear seat and one on the windshield opposite the driver—to help the passenger stay in place at high speeds.

Suspension modifications included a stiffer front stabilizer bar, and the front coil springs and rear leaves were specially modified to keep the car level on the track's steeply banked curves. To handle the 100-plus—miles per hour speeds required for pace car duties, the Mustang pace car was equipped with the High Performance 289 and Borg-Warner transmissions. Benson Ford drove the 1964 Mustang in its first pace car appearance.

Indy 500 officials and the Festival board of directors received 35 additional convertibles to transport beauty queens and use in other publicity events. The parade vehicles were equipped with 289-4V small-block engines. Transmissions varied from four-speed manuals to the Cruise-O-Matic automatic transmissions. The cars were painted white with red, white, and blue interiors. A special blue boot was installed to cover the top when it was folded down. The body's white paint, called Pace Car White, was slightly different from the production Wimbledon White.

Ford built 185 pace car replica Mustang hardtops and used them as dealer sales incentives for their green and checkered flag contests. The checkered flag dealers won a replica car, and green flag dealers won the right to purchase one of the white hardtops. Lee Iacocca presented the winning dealers with their cars on May 14, 1964.

The replicas were painted Pace Car White with white and blue vinyl interior and featured the same lettering and decal packages. All were outfitted with 260-2V V-8 Cruise-O-Matic automatic, and power steering.

After the race, one of the original three pace cars was presented to race winner A. J. Foyt. At this time, the fate of that car and the other two original pace cars is unknown.

Second Time Around Indy 500 1979

In 1979, Ford was selected to pace the 63rd running of the Indianapolis 500. Fifteen years after the debut of the original Mustang, the 1979 model represented a major redesign evolution. Former race car driver Jackie Stewart drove the pace car for Ford.

Ford celebrated the honor and built over 10,000 replica hatchback models. Convertibles were no longer in production. All were painted Silver Metallic with black accents and red/orange striping. The engine options were limited to the Turbo four-cylinder or 302 V-8.

Ford asked performance specialist Jack Roush to build the 1979 pace car 302 V-8 engine. Modifications included high performance camshafts and cylinder heads. Other special equipment on the pace car and replica models included Recaro bucket seats, a black reversed hood scoop, front air dam, rear spoiler, and a T-roof. The pop-up roof was offered as an option on most Mustangs two years later. To improve traction and performance, Ford installed new metric Michelin TRX low-profile tires on cast aluminum wheels. The top of the line Special Suspension package included shock absorber valving and special springs and stabilizers at both ends of the car.

The "official pace car" graphics package included a Indianapolis Motor Speedway logo, a series of three galloping horses, and "official pace car" decals large enough to fill the available space on the side of the car. The decals were installed by the dealer at the buyer's request.

Third Time Around

The Ford Mustang was selected to be the official pace car of the Indianapolis 500 for the third time in 1994. Ford officials invited three drivers to participate in the pre-race driving duties. Alex Trotman, Ford's chairman; four-time Indy 500 winner A. J. Foyt; and Parnelli Jones, also a Indy 500 winner, were selected and circled the track in identical Rio Red Cobras. Parnelli Jones drove pace car to start the 78th annual race.

The pace car Cobras were equipped with an automatic transmission, a special aftermarket roll bar with flashing light unit to communicate with the racers, and a fuel cell. The replica Cobras that were sold to the public were powered by the 240 horsepower 5.0L V-8 engine. A Borg-Warner five-speed manual transmission, performance suspension, and Goodyear radials on 17-inch aluminum wheels completed the package. Like in 1979, a special lettering and decal package was offered as a dealer installed option.

Only 190 Mustang pace cars were built to commemorate the 48th annual Indianapolis 500-mile race. Note how the factory stripe ended at the end of the hood and did not run under the bumper.

Unlike the actual Wimbledon White pace cars used at the Indianapolis Speedway, the vehicles the public bought were painted Pace Car White, paint code C.

Buyers of the 1965 pace car could only acquire the vehicle as a hardtop. Each pace car came with a 260-ci V-8 that generated 164 horsepower.

The exterior paint scheme of white and blue was carried into the 1965 pace car interior. The floor-mounted shifter faux spoke steering wheel lent a sporty air to the pony car.

Contrasting seat belts welcomed drivers to the slip behind the wheel of the 1965 Indy pace car Mustang. Early Mustangs avoided over-styling.

Mustang ran a second stint as Indy 500 pace car in 1979. Approximately 11,000 replicas were sold to the public.

With Michelin TRX low-profile tires and metric cast-aluminum wheels, the 1979 Mustang pace car replica used a special suspension to hold the hatchback flat on the road.

Mustang led the pack again at the 1994 Indy 500 as pace car. The SN-95 restyle saw the return of the non-functional scoop in front of the rear wheels.

Part of the commemorative package on the 1994 Indianapolis Motor Speedway pace car included embroidered leather faced seats.

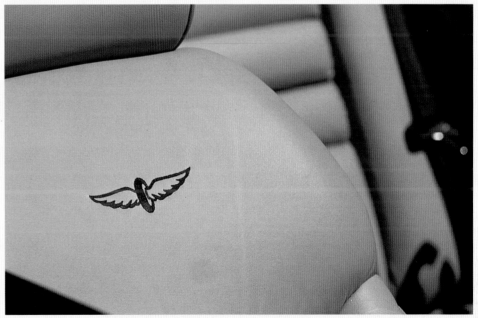

1980
Cobra

In the second year of the new design, very little changed on the hatchback and notchback models. The inside door handles were moved higher on the door panel, and P-metric radial tires, a maintenance-free battery, and halogen headlights were standard on all models.

Options for 1980 included Recaro bucket seats, a roof luggage rack, and lift back louvered windows. A smaller 255-ci V-8 replaced the 302. Horsepower dropped to 119. The 255 was equipped with an automatic transmission. The 2.3L four-cylinder and inline six were offered with a four-speed manual transmission.

Changes to the Cobra were more significant. The Cobra had a new front air dam with integrated fog lamps and a rear facing hood scoop. A new rear spoiler resembled the 1979 pace car design.

On the outside, new pinstripes updated the Cobra's appearance. A black Tu-Tone treatment was used on the body panels, and the quarter windows had striping and COBRA lettering. Dual black sport mirrors, bodyside moldings with color-keyed accent stripes, and chrome exhaust extensions rounded out the 1980 upgrades.

1981

In 1981, Mustang production and sales numbers sagged along the with the rest of the automotive industry. Ford discontinued the Cobra option that year.

The biggest news of the year was the introduction of the T-roof. To support the new roof, Ford engineers modified the chassis with H-shaped reinforcements. The T-roof with two removable tinted glass panels was offered on the two-door or three-door hatchback. The new roof met federal body structure safety regulations.

Other new options included reclining bucket seats, power windows, and a control for the passenger window. New warning lights informed drivers about low fuel and wiper fluid levels.

McLaren Mustang

The McLaren Mustang was offered as a limited edition performance model and resembled the IMSA racing show car. A turbocharged engine delivered 175 horsepower. The McLaren featured a front spoiler, functional hood scoop, and fender flares. Just 250 McLarens were produced and priced at $25,000 each.

1982

After a 12 year absence, the Mustang GT was reintroduced and replaced the Cobra and Ghia models. The GT looked more conservative than the previous snake-striped Cobra. The front grille and spoiler matched the body color.

The 302 V-8, now called the 5.0 liter, came with a two-barrel carburetor, aluminum intake manifold, and better exhaust system. Rear traction bars helped control rear wheel hop. The GT came with a front air dam, rear spoiler, and a front facing non-functional hood scoop.

1983 GT and 1983 Convertible

The nose of the 1983 Mustangs was redesigned to appear rounder and more aerodynamic. At the rear, changes included European-styled new taillights, a rear spoiler influenced by the 1979 pace car, and dual tailpipes.

The Mustang convertible was first introduced to the public at the 1982 Chicago Auto Show and returned to the model lineup in 1983. The convertible started out as a hardtop notchback. The car was manufactured at the Dearborn facility and sent to Cars & Concepts in Brighton, Michigan, for customization. The convertible top and interior trim was added before the convertibles were shipped to dealers for sale. Equipment on the convertible included a power top, glass rear window, and roll-down side windows.

The 1983 Turbo GT Mustang introduced an improved turbocharged 2.3 liter, four-cylinder fuel injected engine. Larger tires improved the GT's handling. The TRX Michelin tires were wider and lower in profile.

The GT featured a rear facing nonfunctioning hood scoop and a wide back stripe that extended through the blacked-out grille. A 5.0 badge announced the new engine on the body side panel behind the front wheels. The Mustang GT was the fastest standard domestic model on the market that year. The GT accelerated from 0 to 60 in under seven seconds.

20th Anniversary

In celebration of the Mustang's 20th birthday, Ford introduced commemorative models. The special editions were available as convertibles and notchbacks and only offered in Oxford White with a Canyon red interior. Only 5,260 20th anniversary models were built. Commemorative models were equipped with either the turbocharged four-cylinder or five-speed 5.0 liter HO.

The 20th anniversary models featured a red GT 350 body panel stripe. The GT 350 label seemed odd since the special edition models celebrated the first Mustang, not the Shelby GT cars that came later. A galloping pony decal was placed on the front fender.

Two commemorative badges were mounted on the dash panels. One was a horseshoe-shaped medallion on the passenger side. A few months after the purchase, the owner received a form to fill out and send in for a second badge. The second medallion said "Limited Edition" with a serial number and the owner's name. To finish the look, Michelin TRX tires were mounted on special aluminum wheels.

1984 Mustang SVO

Ford's Special Vehicle Operations (SVO) was created in 1981 to develop limited edition performance models and supervise Ford's racing operations.

In mid-1984, the Mustang SVO was introduced. It featured a front fascia with integral fog lamps, but no grille. An off-center functional scoop also made the vehicle unique. The first SVO came with a polycarbonate dual-wing rear spoiler standard.

Powered by a 2.3 liter, turbocharged overhead cam four-cylinder engine, the SVO Mustang came with an intercooler and tuned port fuel-injection system. A computer chip controlled all engine functions. A five-speed manual transmission was the only one available for the SVO.

The SVO top-notch handling package included Koni adjustable shocks, four wheel disc brakes, and a Quadra-Shock rear suspension. Goodyear P225/50VR NCT tires were mounted on 16-inch aluminum wheels. The SVO was easy to identify with its unique grille, hood scoop, and rear spoiler.

Inside, the interior matched the SVO name. Features included a Hurst shifter, adjustable Recaro bucket seats, leather-wrapped steering wheel, premium stereo system, and for the aggressive performance driver, a dead pedal for the driver's left foot.

The SVO options list was limited to air conditioning, power windows and locks, cassette stereo, pop-up sunroof, and leather seats.

The 1984 SVO Mustang was very well received. *Motor Trend* called the SVO, "the best driving street Mustang the factory has ever produced."

With only 145 horsepower on tap, the P220/55R390 Michelin TRX tires mounted on the 1984 20th Anniversary Edition Turbo GT 350 weren't at serious risk.

Only 600 ragtop GT Turbo Mustangs were sold in 1984. The soft sales prompted Ford to pull the plug on the model after only two years.

Federal regulations mandated that speedometers stop their numbers at 85 miles per hour, but the 1984 Mustang GT Turbo had little problem swinging the needle far past that limit.

Left: Only 104 20th Anniversary Edition Turbo GT 350 convertibles were built in 1984 and sold for $13,441. The buyer got only 145 horsepower and 180 foot-pounds of torque.

1984

The 1984 Mustang SVO was named after the group that created it—Special Vehicle Operations. Horsepower was rated at 175, which was enough to move from 0 to 60 miles per hour in 7.5 seconds.

A smooth nose used only on the 1984 Mustang SVO model was part of the reason the vehicle cost close to $17,000. Top speed was 128 miles per hour, but the aerodynamic aids imparted stability at speed.

The unique biplane rear spoiler used the upper wing to force passing air to tumble onto the lower portion to create downforce.

Below: Graceful biplane rear spoiler on the 1984 Mustang SVO was first seen on the European XR4i Sierra. Cleaning under the spoiler posed a challenge.

Below: The offset functional hood scoop fed outside air directly through the air-to-air intercooler, part of the equation used to extract 174 horsepower from only 2.3L.

1985

All 1985 models received an updated front-end design with an integrated air dam and rectangular parking lights. A Ford oval was displayed in the center of the grille panel. The taillights extended the full width of the car for the first time. New flush-mounted headlights that used separate bulb and lens/reflector systems were installed in 1985 SVO models. The Goodyear Eagle Gatorbacks mounted on 15x7 aluminum wheels were wider than any other previous Mustang tire specification.

The standard engine was the 2.3 liter, four-cylinder with the 3.8L V-6 and 5.0L HO V-8 as available options. The 1985 GT engine received a new accessory belt drive and a high performance camshaft. Combined with new stainless-steel headers mated to a dual exhaust system, engine performance increased to 210 horsepower.

A limited edition Mustang model called the Ninety Twister II was sold in the Kansas City sales district in 1985. They were available as three-door and convertible GTs. The only difference from standard Mustangs was an exterior graphics package and dash badge. The Twister IIs came in Bright Red, Medium Canyon Red, Oxford White, and Silver Metallic.

1986
Mustang SVO

Overall, the model lineup was simplified. The GT was now offered in a three-door hatchback or convertible. The LX Mustangs could be ordered in a two-door, three-door, or convertible. The limited number of options and models continued in the coming years.

Other than minor trim and color changes, the 1985 and 1986 models were almost identical. In 1986 a new brake light was installed in the rear spoiler. The Center High-Mounted Stoplight is the best way to tell the two years apart.

Priced about $2,500 more than a 5.0L GT, the SVO production numbers were relatively small, with a total of 9,844 units from 1984 to 1986.

The last SVO went out in style. Goodyear tires were mounted on 16-inch aerodynamic slotted wheels. Koni shocks front and rear improved handling performance.

The three-year run of high-performance Mustang SVO models came to an end in 1986.

1987

After a decade with the same basic design, the 1987 Mustang received a major facelift. The grille and front bumper were changed to an integrated smooth aerodynamic look similar to other Ford models.

Since the SVO model was no longer offered, the GT became the top performance model. The 1987 GT received a new nose with flush fitting headlamps and an updated interior. The new dash instrument panel included gauges for fuel, water temperature, oil pressure, voltmeter, tachometer, and a 85-miles-per-hour speedometer. New articulated seats with power lumbar support and thigh support were standard. The GT's suspension was improved with many parts and assemblies from the previous SVO models.

A ground effects skirt package came with a front air dam with integrated fog lamps, air scoops in front of each wheel, lower body side rocker panels, and a rear valance.

1988–1989

After the 1987 redesign, the Mustang remained relatively unchanged the last two years of the 1980s. In 1989, the LX was called the LX 5.0L Sport when equipped with the V-8 engine. The Sport model used the adjustable front seats previously available only on the GT.

Ford engineers redesigned the air intake systems to increase engine performance. The system that replaced the existing speed density air measurement intake was called Mass Air. The new system read the air intake more accurately and was easier to modify for the aftermarket and performance buffs.

In 1989, a small token to performance was made when the standard 85-miles-per-hour speedometer was replaced with a 140-miles-per-hour version.

The 25th Anniversary

The 25th anniversary of the Mustang was debated and understated. Was the anniversary in 1989 25 years after the first 1964–1/2 Mustang was introduced? Other managers suggested the birthday should be in 1990 to commemorate the first full year of sales, but the decision was to hold the anniversary in 1989.

Mustangs built between April 17, 1989, and April 17, 1990, came with a special commemorative running pony medallion on the dashboard.

More bang for the buck was the rallying cry when the 1987 Mustang GT hit the pavement. With a sport suspension, aggressive looks, and a 225 horsepower V-8, the starting price of $12,106 was value rich.

The Mustang SVO was one of the first vehicles to incorporate the majority of cooling air that entered the radiator from underneath the front bumper.

Loads of power at moderate cost was the hallmark of the durable 5.0L engine. Using throttle-body electronic fuel injection, the 90-degree V-8 was rated at 225 horsepower.

Steve Saleen built just 160 Saleen SSCs in 1989. Equipped with 16-inch wheels on a stiffened chassis and Monroe adjustable shock absorbers, the 292 horsepower street fighter topped out at 156 miles per hour.

Ford changed the method of rating engine output in 1993, which resulted in the 5.0L V-8 coming in at 205 horsepower, down 20 from the year before.

Flush headlights and grille aided the 1993 Mustang's CD, rated at 0.39. The last year before a major restyle, the 1993 Mustang posted impressive sales of 114,228 units.

1990–1993

In 1990, the Fox platform entered its 12th season. No significant mechanical or design changes were made for the 1990 model year. This trend remained until the next generation Mustang was introduced in 1994. Styling changes were so minimal that Mustang brochures used most of the same photography in 1991 and 1992.

Driver side airbags appeared on 1991 models, but passenger side airbags had to wait a few years. There was no incentive to redesign the dash with a new model just a few years away.

Ford celebrated the Mustang's birthday with a limited edition LX 5.0L Sport convertible. This Mustang was painted Emerald Green metallic and equipped with a white leather interior and white top. The 25th anniversary edition used the GT model's spoked aluminum wheels.

Mustang sales declined during this time period and dropped under 100,000 units sold for the first time in several years, with less than 80,000 Mustangs were sold in 1992.

Limited edition models with special colors and option packages were offered in 1992 and 1993 to help dealers jump start sales. Convertibles in Vibrant Red and Bright Yellow were built in small numbers. Color-keyed body side moldings and bumpers made the convertibles stand out in a crowd.

1990–1993

Ford's Special Vehicle Team (SVT) introduced the 1993 Cobra, the last high-performance Mustang based on the Fox platform, at the 1992 Chicago Auto Show.

To differentiate the Cobra from the GT, side skirts, rear wing, 17-inch, 7-spoke aluminum alloy wheels, and a restyled front valance were used. The familiar running horse reappeared in the grille treament. Engine modifications boosted the horsepower rating to 235 horsepower.

The Cobra's suspension was upgraded to improve handling. Softer rear springs, an anti-sway bar, and wide Goodyear tires made the Cobra's ride smooth and comfortable.

Cobra R

Fulfilling its mission to build high-performance and racing models, the SVT built a limited number of 1993 Cobra R road racing cars.

Mechanically similar to the street version, the SVT Cobra R was stripped of anything that added weight to the car, including the rear seat, sound insulation, and radio. The stock suspension was replaced with firmer springs and upgraded shocks and struts.

Only 107 Cobra R models were produced, and they were sold-out before production was completed. Since the car was intended for racing, most of the R models were purchased by collectors.

By 1991, the Mustang's Fox chassis was getting long in the tooth, but annual improvements and upgrades kept the 25th anniversary models rolling briskly out of showrooms.

1994

As the 1980s came to a close, new government safety regulations and fuel economy standards spelled the end of the Fox platform Mustang.

Dedicated Ford project managers and engineers worked long hours to develop the fourth-generation Mustang. Called the SN95, the new car was inspired by the Mach III concept car displayed at auto shows in 1992.

Using engine components and chassis assemblies from other Ford models, the new rear drive, front engine platform was called the Fox-4. The fourth-generation Mustang was more aerodynamic, quieter, and completely modernized.

Classic Mustang design elements were incorporated throughout the car, though. The sleek hood, angled windshield, and short rear deck brought back memories of earlier models. The galloping pony badge returned to the black grille. Air vents in front of the rear tires and a small hood scoop were definite reminders of past Mustangs. The only design element that wasn't well received was the three level rear taillights.

The interior was completely redesigned in 1994. It resembled a close-fitting cockpit. Standard equipment included dual air bags, power driver's seat, and a tilt steering wheel. A Mach 460 sound system provided music for the road.

1995

In the second year of new design, the GTS coupe was added to the model lineup. The GTS was positioned between the base Mustang and the GT. The GTS coupe was equipped with the 5.0L High Output engine, a stainless-steel exhaust system, and 16-inch, 5-spoke cast aluminum wheels.

The Special Vehicle Team introduced a new Cobra R racing model in 1995. Built for stock racing, the Cobra R was equipped with a 300 horsepower, 5.8L, 351-ci V-8 engine. Race-ready specifications included a Tremec five-speed transmission, heavy duty radiator, and oil cooler. Goodrich Comp T/A tires, a special fiberglass hood, and a larger 20-gallon gas tank were part of the race package. Like the earlier R model, the 1995 Cobra R did not have a rear seat, air conditioning, power accessories, or fog lights. The Cobra R was available only in white.

To keep the 250 Cobra R models in the hands of racers instead of collectors, buyers needed a competition license from a sanctioned racing organization to qualify.

Three-element taillights continued to make an appearance on the 1994 Mustang. Dual exhausts let the 5.0L, 240 horsepower V-8 of this Cobra convertible breathe.

The last year for the 5.0L V-8 was 1995. The GT enjoyed its 215 horsepower, but a modular 4.6L SOHC V-8 was slipped in the following year, rated at 260 horsepower.

The base price for a 1995 Mustang GT Coupe was $18,105, and 17-inch wheels went for $380. The rear spoiler was part of the GT package.

1996 | After just one year of availability, the GTS was discontinued. The base, convertible, and GT models returned. Engine modifications were the biggest changes in 1996. The 5.0L V-8 used in the past was replaced with a 4.6L V-8. The new engine was a single overhead cam SOHC design that improved low-end torque and overall performance. The new engine was mated with a new Borg-Warner five-speed transmission.

The SVT Cobra | The Special Vehicle Team introduced a SVT Cobra convertible in the spring of 1996. Powered by the new 4.6L SOHC engine, the SVT was one of the fastest Mustangs in recent years and covered a quarter-mile in less than 13 seconds.

The majority of buyers ordered the optional leather seats and rear spoiler. The front grille featured a coiled Cobra snake badge instead of the galloping pony used in 1995.

1997–1998 | For the next two years, the Mustang changed very little. The body style remained unchanged. A Passive Anti-Theft System was first offered as an option on the 1996 GT and Cobra models. It was standard on all 1997 models and used an encoded ignition key that disabled the engine if the key transponder code didn't match the code in the car's computerized control system.

Minor revisions were made to the interior. The GT received a new flecked seat pattern. Mustangs with automatic transmissions came with a new shifter. In 1998, the clock was removed from the instrument panel and integrated into the radio tuning display.

The GT Sport Group was offered as an option in 1998 and included a new hood, wraparound fender stripes, a leather-wrapped steering wheel, and 16-inch cast aluminum wheels.

Tommy Kendall, driving a Mustang Cobra in the Trans-Am racing series, set a record with 11 consecutive victories on the way to winning the 1997 Trans–Am racing championship.

Upper right: Weighing 3,365 pounds, the 1994 Cobra was designed by Bud Magaldi and based on a concept vehicle nicknamed "Arnold Schwarzenegger." *Randy Leffingwell*

Right: For 1996, the Mustang Cobra used a 4.6L DOHC V-8 to generate 305 horsepower and special Mystic paint to turn heads. The colors changed as the viewer walked around the vehicle. The finish was only offered on the Cobra.

SVT (Special Vehicle Team) was a descendent of the original SVO (Special Vehicle Operations). Intended to develop high-performance versions of mainstream Ford products, it was a lean team that injects excitement into the entire lineup.

In 1998, Ford sold 5,174 Cobra coupes, which started at $25,710. That sum bought a 4.6L DOHC 305 horsepower V-8 and unique circular fog lamps.

1999 Mustang

Call it evolution instead of revolution. In 1999, the 35th anniversary of the Mustang, it received another design update. The rounded lines of the 1994 to 1998–era were replaced by sharper, crisper lines and creases. The only body surface that remained unchanged was the roofline.

Slightly longer and wider, the 1999 Mustang received upgrades and modifications in every area. The V-6 engine performance received a new intake manifold and cylinder head improvements. The 4.6L V-8 was also upgraded with a new camshaft, valves, and an intake manifold of its own.

Changes to the body included a nonfunctional hood scoop and a rear deck lid made of a sheet molded compound to save weight. Inside, the driver's seat received one more inch of travel adjustment, and new fabrics and patterns were offered.

For the first time, the Mustang could be ordered with an optional all-speed traction control system. The Bosch system used ABS sensors to detect wheel slip and reduce engine power by retarding the spark and cutting fuel to as many as six of the eight cylinders. Braking power was automatically applied to the drive wheels.

Chassis improvements included a new floorpan, frame braces to reduce vibration on the convertible model, and the addition of soundproofing materials on the rocker panels to reduce noise.

The 35th Anniversary Mustang

The 35th Anniversary Mustang was only available as a GT model. It had blacked-out trim and a unique silver and black leather interior. The silver exterior featured a nonfunctional hood scoop. A honeycombed mesh similar to the front grille was inside the scoop. A rear spoiler was part of the limited edition package.

To celebrate the Mustang's early heritage, the grille carried a tri-color pony emblem that hadn't been seen since 1968.

All 1999 Mustangs, including the 35th Anniversary Limited Edition, carried a special badge on the front fenders. The Limited Edition featured the same 17-inch wheels that were optional on the GT.

SVT Cobra 1999

In addition to the changes made to the 1999 Mustangs, the SVT Cobra received new round fog lights in the front fascia. The Cobra's hood did not come with the fake scoop found on the other models.

A new independent rear suspension system was the most important change for the 1999 SVT Cobra. Adapted from the Lincoln Mark VIII, the system used a series of new control arms mounted to a tubular subframe. The result was much better handling and control.

The interior was dressed in Dark Charcoal or Medium Parchment leather. Cloth upholstery wasn't offered as an option in 1999.

On August 6, 1999, Ford directly told dealers to stop selling the SVT Cobra. The unsold inventory was returned to Ford for engine improvements. Ford replaced the intake manifold, exhaust system, and the computerized engine management controls. The Cobra returned to the Mustang lineup in 2001.

2000 Saleen

In 2000, the Mustang line remained relatively unchanged. Performance fans didn't have to look far to find a Mustang worthy to take on the competition.

Like Carroll Shelby before him, Steve Saleen took stock Mustangs and made them gallop faster. Introduced in 1984, the first Saleen Mustang modifications were limited to aerodynamic bodywork and suspension components. Engine modifications were eventually added.

The 2000 S281-SC is a good example of the Saleen modifications. Exterior touches like an optional lightweight hood, rear spoiler, 18-inch chrome-plated wheels, and ground-hugging front valance and rocker panels gave the car an aggressive look. Saleen lettering on the lower door panel identified the car as not your usual Mustang.

The 4.6L DOHC engine was supercharged matched with a five-speed manual transmission and dual exhaust. Equipped with top of the line Pirelli ZR tires the 360 horsepower Saleen was capable of moving from 0 to 60 in 4.8 seconds.

With a base price of $28,950, the Saleen was well equipped with air conditioning, cruise control, power brakes and locks, bucket seats, and a powerful sound system. Popular options included anti-lock brakes and leather seats.

Although the stock Mustang was modified extensively, buyers received full warranty protection from Ford.

The splitter is a race car–derived piece that could be removed for daily street use by twisting the Dzus fasteners and pulling the item away from the vehicle. The splitter is mandatory for track use.

Opposite page: Tall rear spoiler is part of the 2000 Cobra R's aero package, necessary when the top speed is 186 miles per hour. Child seat anchors on the package shelf were retained from regular Mustangs, and there was no rear seat.

The Mustang came out looking for big game in 2000 with the release of the Cobra R, which was a thinly disguised race car legalized for use on the street. With a 385 horsepower 5.4L DOHC V-8, six-speed manual transmission, independent rear suspension, and massive 265/40ZR-18 BF Goodrich g-Force tires, the Cobra R generates a 0 to 60–miles–per–hour time of only 4.8 seconds.

Bullitt
1968–2000

1968 Ford Mustang Fastback Stars in *Bullitt*

In 1968, a Mustang fastback co-starred with Steve McQueen in the movie *Bullitt*. McQueen played Lt. Frank Bullitt, and the action scenes left the audience breathless. To this day, car and movie fans alike agree that the high-speed car chase scene through the streets of San Francisco in one the best chases in movie history.

Before filming started, Warner Brothers selected two Mustang fastbacks. Max Balchowski, a well-known race driver and engine builder, was hired to modify the cars for the high-speed chase scenes. In ten days, Balchowski modified the 390-ci V-8 engine, created braces for the front fenders, and upgraded the suspension. To handle the twists and turns, he added stronger springs and Koni shock absorbers.

During the filming of the chase scenes, one of the cars was extensively damaged. After the movie was filmed, Warner Brothers sent the broken car to the crusher and sold the backup to an employee in its editing department.

In 1974, the Mustang featured in *Bullitt* was offered for sale in *Road & Track* magazine. It was reported that Steve McQueen wanted to purchase the car for his own collection. When he found out the car was already sold, he sought out the newest owner and was turned down.

At this writing, the original *Bullitt* movie car is stored at a farm in the Ohio River Valley. It's been years since the powerful car has been driven, and the current owner has declined recent offers to buy and restore the car.

The Bullitt Returns
in 2001

Ford presented an updated Bullitt concept car at the 2000 Los Angeles Auto Show. The reaction was so positive Ford included the Bullitt in the 2001 model line. Based on performance levels, the 2001 Bullitt fits between the Mustang GT and SVT Cobra. The 2001 Bullitt sticker read $26,830, which was $3,600 more than the GT.

The new Bullitt is based on the 2001 Ford Mustang GT coupe. It was built on the same Dearborn Assembly Plant production line as the GT, and only 6,500 Bullitts were produced. Each Bullitt came with a specialized serialized identification label that was attached at the factory. Exterior colors for the Bullitt included the Dark Highland Green seen on the original movie car and True Blue and Black.

On the outside, the 2001 Bullitt featured design elements reminiscent of the original 1968 fastback movie car. The C-pillars and quarter-panel molding have been modified to reflect the original model. Other exterior features included side scoops, 17-inch Bullitt-style aluminum wheels, and a brushed aluminum fuel filler door on the rear quarter panel.

The Bullitt GT is powered by a 4.6L SOHC V-8. At 270 horsepower, the Bullitt engine delivered significantly more torque than the Mustang GT engine. The exhaust system featured high flow mufflers with an aggressive performance sound that brings back memories of the *Bullitt* soundtrack.

Happiest on a rac track, the 2000 Mustang Cobra R was built in limited numbers and went for a lofty sum of $55,000. Devoid of air conditioning, a radio, or a back seat, it was intended for enthusiast driving, period.

Designed to perform on the streets, the Bullitt's suspension was lowered 3/4-inch. The suspension performance package included front and rear stabilizer bars, frame rail connectors, and Tokico struts and shocks. The 13-inch Brembo brake calipers were painted red and could be seen through the spokes of the 17-inch wheels. Steve McQueen would feel right at home at the wheel of the new Bullitt.

2001 SVT Cobra and 2001 GT

Mention the words muscle car and most people think of Mustangs like the Mach 1, Shelby Cobra, and Boss 302. In 2001, the SVT Cobra lived up to the Mustang performance reputation when those earlier models ruled the streets.

The hood, front fascia, air vents, and special coiled snake badges gave the Cobra a distinctive look. At the rear, Cobra lettering was molded into the rear body panels. Tri-color taillamps, an optional rear spoiler, and polished exhaust pipes finished the look.

The interior never let the driver forget they were driving a Cobra. Its emblems were embroidered on the seats. Interior features included a leather-wrapped steering wheel and shift knob, tilt steering, power windows, door locks, SecuriLock anti-theft system, and six-disc CD player.

The SVT Cobra's sophisticated 4.6L, DOHC V-8 engine was hand built on the Niche Line at Ford's Romeo, Michigan, engine plant. Specially trained two-man teams moved along ten stations to build one engine every hour. Combined with a Tremec five-speed manual transmission the 320 horsepower SVT Cobra went from 0 to 60 miles per hour in 5.6 seconds and traveled a quarter-mile in 14.2 seconds at 99.7 miles per hour.

To keep that power under control, the SVT Cobra was equipped with an all-speed traction control system as standard equipment. Not every piece of safety equipment was as this sophisticated. The 2001 SVT Cobra was equipped with a BeltMinder safety belt that warned drivers to buckle up. If they didn't, a warning bell rang out and a red light flashed on the instrument panel. Another light warned of a loose gas cap.

2001 GT

Traditionally, the GT designation positioned the car at the top of the Mustang line. Usually equipped with luxury appointments and standard features to keep the driver comfortable on the road, performance certainly wasn't sacrificed. The 2001 GT didn't let anyone forget that high performance was part of its heritage.

Updated in 1999, the GT received design upgrades included shaded headlamp lenses, and nonfunctional air scoops near the rear wheels and on the hood. Seventeen-inch, five-spoke wheels were standard. The Premium edition added the special wheels used on the Bullitt Limited edition and a six-disc CD player.

While the 2001 Mustang GT convertible was a very mild evolution of the previous year, its aggressive stance helped to sell 18,336 units.

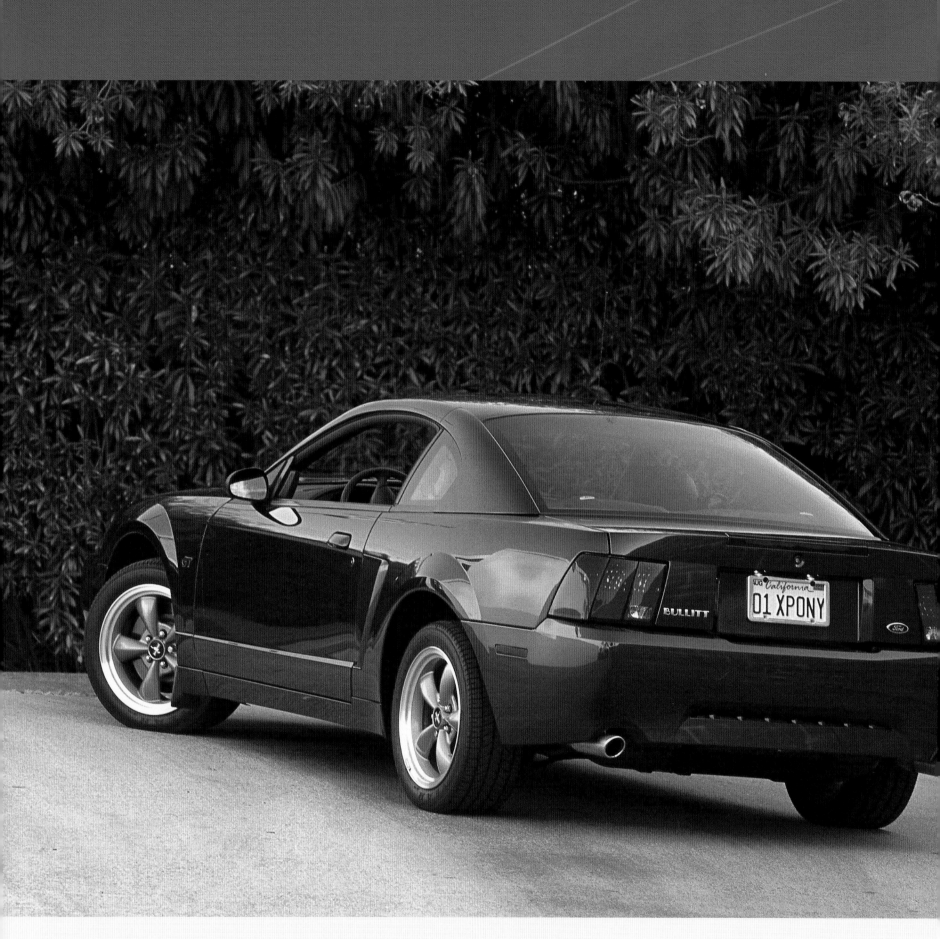

For the first time, Ford named a special Mustang after a movie. In 1968, Steve McQueen starred in *Bullitt* that featured a 1968 fastback. The movie and car achieved cult status, and Ford rode that wave by releasing the limited edition Bullitt.

Instrumentation on the 2001 Mustang GT was clear and easy to read. The 4.6L 260 horsepower could coax the speedometer needle into the upper range of the dial.

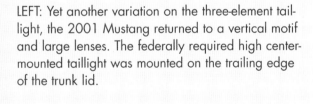

LEFT: Yet another variation on the three-element tail-light, the 2001 Mustang returned to a vertical motif and large lenses. The federally required high center-mounted taillight was mounted on the trailing edge of the trunk lid.

Replicating the script found on the instrument panel of a 1968 Mustang, the 2001 Bullitt packed 265 horsepower under the hood and Torq-Thrust–style wheels at each corner.

2002 Mustang

In 2002, the Mustang was available in coupe and convertible body styles. Standard, Deluxe, and Premium packages were offered for each model. The addition of the new SVT Cobra coupe and convertible made headlines in the automotive enthusiast magazines.

The standard equipment list included air conditioning, power windows and door locks, tilt steering, and a remote keyless entry system. The SecuriLock theft deterrent system prevents the car from being started without a properly coded key. Safety features like anti-lock brakes, traction control, three-point seatbelts, and driver and passenger air bags helped the Mustang receive a five-star front crash test rating.

The 3.8L 193 horsepower V-6 was the standard engine for the base coupe and convertible models. The GT coupe and convertible received the optional 4.6L V-8 that delivered 260 horsepower.

Music has always been part of the driving experience, and in 2002, Ford installed a state-of-the-art sound system in the Mustang. The Mach 1000 system featured a six-disc CD changer that used six amplifiers to deliver the driver's favorite songs. An optional MP3 player was also offered.

The convertible's power top was equipped with a scratch-resistant glass rear window. A special boot protected the folded fabric top and gave it a clean look.

The new 2002 SVT Cobra received a new exterior appearance package. The new front bumper, grille opening, driving lamps, side scoops, and rear spoiler led a long list of upgrades. The hood featured two rear-facing vents and was significantly redesigned to accommodate the supercharger on the engine.

The Cobra's cast-iron block 4.6L DOHC V-8 delivered 390 horsepower. An Eaton supercharger improved acceleration and performance. A Tremec six-speed manual transmission shifted the power to 17-inch wheels.

As the top of the line Mustang, the interior lived up to its position. The illuminated instrument cluster used titanium faces and included a boost gauge to track the supercharger operation. A leather-wrapped gearshift and steering wheel, power windows, door locks, mirrors, and trunk release completed the luxury interior package.

The 40th Anniversary Mustang

Forty years ago, Ford brought editors and writers to New York to give them the first look at the 1964-1/2 Mustang. The buzz created by the media coverage led to huge crowds at Ford dealers. As the 40th anniversary nears, the anticipation is building.

The first pony car was followed by competitors and imitators with names such as Camaro, Firebird, Cougar, Barracuda, Challenger, and Javelin. Although most of those names are gone, the Ford Mustang is about to celebrate its 40th anniversary.

In four decades, the management of Ford Motor Company has upgraded, revised, and redesigned the Mustang from top to bottom several times. With the last major redesign in 1999, Mustang enthusiasts are anxiously awaiting the introduction of special 40th anniversary editions and a glimpse of what the future holds for the original pony car.

It's fitting that Ford returned to New York in April 2003 to give the automotive press the first glimpse at the 40th anniversary limited editions. The design of the special cars is reminiscent of the Mustang muscle cars of the 1967 to 1970 era.

Available in late 2003, the 40th Anniversary Edition package will be available on Mustang GT coupes and convertibles. A reported 5,700 anniversary models will be built.

Like the Mustangs of the past, the new models will be built on platforms used by other Ford nameplates. First the Falcon, Fairmont, Fox, and now the DEW. The DEW platform is also used for the Lincoln, Thunderbird, and Jaguar S-Type. Mustang production will move from Dearborn to Flat Rock, Michigan, to maintain the highest fit and finish standards.

The SVT Mustang Cobra will feature a supercharged 390 horsepower powerplant. Before buyers even consider the engine, they will be captured by the new MystiChrome color-shifting paint. Depending on your eye's viewing angle, the car's color will change from topaz green to cobalt blue to royal purple to deep onyx black. Interior accents will also use the special paint. In 2004, the MystiChrome appearance package will be offered on 1,000 Cobra coupes and convertibles.

The 2004 Mach 1 will also appear as a anniversary edition. The 2004 Mach 1 will come with a 305 horsepower V-8 engine and a ram-air shaker hood scoop that will remind enthusiasts of the original Mach 1. Other features include comfort-weave black leather seats reminiscent of the first model and 17-inch, 5-spoke Heritage wheels. Production will be limited to 5,000 units.

If you're a Mustang fan, the 40th anniversary editions are made for you. With styling and design reminiscent of the glory days combined with the latest engine and suspension technology, the new pony car is ready to gallop.

The Mach 1 returned in 2003, complete with door sill stripe, rear spoiler, and 1970-era script.

Left: The majority of Mustangs sold in model year 2002 packed the 3.8L V-6 under the hood. It generated 190 horsepower and 225 foot-pounds of torque and provided spirited performance.

The 2003 Mustang Mach 1 boasted a functional Shaker hood scoop that fed outside air to the induction system of the 4.6L DOHC V-8 that generated 305 horsepower and 320 foot-pounds of torque.

Grabber Blue was a popular Mustang color in the early 1970s. It returned to the lineup in 2003 on the Mach 1. The taut dimensions of the platform are evident in an overhead view.

The Ford Living Legends program that created Mustangs such as the 2002 Bullitt and 2003 Mach 1 have not stopped at the exterior. Note the Comfortweave upholstery in the 2003 Mach 1.

Mustang 2004 and Beyond

Ford celebrates the 40th anniversary of the Mustang in 2004. Sales of the limited edition models will likely match the enthusiastic response of the first Mustang, but the real news lies one year later when Ford will introduce a completely new Mustang.

What will it look like? Will it be a retro design inspired by the original, or a futurist interpretation of what the first design and engineering team would have created if today's technology and materials were available to them?

It's likely the 40th anniversary edition will be unveiled in January 2004 at the North American International Auto Show in Detroit. The buzz has already begun. Websites devoted to Mustangs are posting spy photos. Enthusiast magazines are publishing interviews with Ford executives that hint at body configurations and engine specifications, and concept cars displayed at consumer auto shows fuel the debate and speculation.

According to the automotive trade press reports in the summer of 2003, concept cars shown at 2003 auto shows in Detroit, Los Angeles, and New York offer a glimpse of what's to come. Presented with a two-seat cockpit, the new Mustang will continue to offer a rear seat configuration. The line is expected to include a GT, convertible, and high performance SVT Cobra.

As in the past, optional engine and handling packages will satisfy every kind of Mustang buyer from luxury cruiser to high-performance street racer.

The new Mustang will take its styling cues from the muscle car Mustangs from the late 1960s and early 1970s. The fastback roofline and quarter window are similar to the 1966 Shelby GT 350. The grille is reminiscent of the 1967–1968 egg crate pattern. The nose design reflects the aggressive stance of the 1969–1970 models.

Built on a modified Thunderbird/Lincoln LS/Jaguar S type platform, the new Mustang's chassis will be lighter, stronger, and deliver better handling and less noise and vibration. New engine and transmission combinations are certain to improve performance over current models with numbers such as 0 to 60 in less than five seconds.

The newest Mustang will be at dealers in the summer of 2004.

The next generation of Mustang will debut as a 2005 model in two body styles, fastback and convertible. This concept was first shown at the 2003 North American International Auto Show in Detroit, Michigan.

Designed at Ford's California Concept Center, the 2005 Mustang employs styling cues from a wide range of Mustangs and Shelbys to create a pony car for the next millennium.

Retaining the Mustang's three-element taillight motif, the 2005 Mustang uses the center-mounted fuel filler cap, similar to the installation used in Mustang's first ten years.

While the instrument panel gives off a retro feel, it is chock full of contemporary electronics. The 2005 Mustang GT is expected to pack 400 horsepower using a supercharged V-8.

Production 2005 Mustangs will have six inches in length added between the firewall and front wheel center to increase interior space and improve overall vehicle proportions.

Carroll Shelby had a well-deserved reputation as a race driver and car builder. He should also be remembered as an expert marketer.

From the dramatic striping to the Cobra emblems, Shelby Mustangs always stood out from the crowd of muscle cars. To promote his cars, Shelby created postcards for each model and asked dealers to send them to prospective buyers. Today, collectors covet these cards.

After Shelby sold his cars, he pitched parts and accessories. The Shelby Parts and Accessories catalog included a variety of Shelby and Cobra logo items including plates, beer mugs, ash trays, and cocktail glasses. That was just for the den.

A line of Shelby driving apparel included jackets, driving gloves, hats, sweatshirts, T-shirts, decals, and a Snell-approved driving helmet. Shelby even sold a deodorant called Pit Stop—"A real man's deodorant."

When the Mustang was introduced, three engine options were offered. The standard 101 horsepower, 170-ci, six-cylinder and two small-block V-8s: the 164 horsepower 260 and the 289 4V with 210 horsepower. A larger 200-ci, six-cylinder replaced the original 170-ci engine in the fall of 1964. Approximately 30 percent of the Mustangs sold in the first five years had the six-cylinder engine installed.

The basic six was available with a single barrel carburetor and offered with three- or four-speed manual transmissions. An automatic transmission was also available.

The first V-8 powerplant offered for the Mustang was the 260-ci engine with a two barrel carburetor that was only offered in the 1964-1/2 model. The engine used a generator. To charge the battery, Ford switched to an alternator on models built later in the first year of production.

1965

The Challenger 289 V-8 was available with an optional four-barrel carburetor. The engine was rated at 225 horsepower and required premium fuel.

Mustangs equipped with the 289 carried a badge on the fender. The 289 was one of Ford's best engines. It weighed around 450 pounds and was powerful and compact. The basic engine is still in use today.

1965 Hi-Po Engine

Mustang owners who wanted performance ordered the 289-ci, V-8 Hi-Po engine. Equipped with an Autolite four-barrel carburetor, the engine delivered 271 horsepower.

Big block engines were slipped into the Mustang in 1967, and with 320 horsepower and 427 foot-pounds of torque, the biggest problem was getting traction.

Shelby never missed a chance to promote his products, such as the classy shifter knob on the 1968 GT 500KR. It used the color scheme from the original GT 350, which in turn used the traditional American racing colors.

At the peak of Shelby's popularity, the accessory catalog was included in Sears and J.C. Penney catalogs. Shelby also marketed engine performance parts with names like the Sidewinder Induction System and the Le Mans Kinetic Superflow Solid Lifter Camshaft Kit. Shelby sold engine parts such as aluminum valve covers, tachometers, intake manifolds, and exhaust headers by mail order. Shelby or CS logos covered everything.

If you couldn't afford a real Shelby GT 350, you could always buy a toy model. Every Shelby built was recreated as a plastic model or diecast replica. Monogram sold a copy of the 1966 Mustang GT 350H model Shelby produced for Hertz.

The Hi-Po name appears on the side emblem of all Mustangs equipped with the powerful engine. Chrome air cleaner and valve covers distinguish the Hi-Po engine from other options.

1967
The 390
Mustang owners demanded performance, power, and speed, and Ford delivered. The 390 big block was used in the Thunderbird, and Ford modified the Mustang to accommodate the engine.

Engineers had to change the position of the shock towers to add more side-to-side room for the engine. Equipped with a four-barrel carburetor, the 390 GT V-8 was rated at 320 horsepower. This was enough power to push the driver back in his seat when the accelerator was floored.

The 428-ci Cobra Jet was built with a collection of existing Ford engine components. The standard version produced 335 horsepower, while the KR performance package, fitted with an oversized intake manifold and Holley carburetor, pushed the engine output to 400 horsepower. The Cobra Jet came with a four-speed manual transmission or an automatic transmission.

Hot Rod magazine tested a Mustang equipped with the Cobra Jet. It went from 0 to 60 in 5.9 seconds and covered a quarter-mile in 13.5 seconds.

Mustang 302
In mid-1968 Ford replaced the 289 with a 302-ci V-8. Using a Autolite four-barrel carburetor, the 302 delivered 230 horsepower, which was 35 more than the 289. The 302 remained in the Mustang's engine list until 1973.

Ford's venerable small-block V-8 displaced 289 cubic inches in 1967, with power outputs between 200 to 271 horsepower, depending on options such as carburetion and camshaft.

Boss 429

This engine was built to comply with NASCAR racing requirements. The 429 V-8 was so big Ford had to move the shock towers another one inch farther apart. The battery was moved to the trunk to make more room. The 429 V-8 was rated at 375 horsepower, but experienced racing mechanics could coax more than 500 horsepower out of the big powerplant. A Holley four-barrel carburetor was standard.

351 Cleveland in 1969

Built at Ford's Windsor, Ohio, plant, the 351W was as a modified version of the existing 302 and available in two- and four-barrel options. The Windsor-based V-8 was used until 1996. The 285 horsepower version was the optional small-block V-8 for the 1971 Mach 1. The stronger 330 horsepower version was only available on the Boss 351.

1974

When Ford introduced the new Mustang II in 1974, a new engine was included. The base 140-ci 2.3L four-cylinder was the first metric American-built engine. Rated at only 88 horsepower, the engine was built for fuel economy instead of street performance.

A German built 171-ci 2.8L V-6 was also offered in 1974 and was the standard in the Mach 1, though available as an option for other models. The V-6 still couldn't match the performance output of past engines.

1975

By this time, engines were measured in metric terms. The 5.0 L V-8 was stuffed into the Mustang II in 1975. With this engine, a driver could cover the quarter-mile in 16.5 seconds at over 80 miles per hour.

In 1979, the 5.0 L 302-ci engine produced just 140 horsepower. In these times, engine performance was measured by clean air standards and fuel economy rather than fast times in the quarter-mile.

1983

The 5.0L HO (High Output) engine improved Mustang's performance. The addition of a Holley four-barrel carburetor improved the horsepower rating to a respectable 175.

1984

Performance was the mission of Ford's Special Vehicle Operations. The Mustang SVO came with just one engine option. A 2.3L four cylinder Turbo. Small but powerful, the engine started with a 175 horsepower rating. The horsepower jumped to 205 in late 1985 after the engine was modified with a turbocharger and intercooler.

In 1968, the Mustang California Special could be purchased with any size engine, such as this 390-ci example, fitted with aftermarket Shelby dress-up parts.

Only two engines were offered in non-Cobra Mustangs in 1993. A 105 horsepower inline four-cylinder and this 5.0L V-8 churned out 205 horses.

RIGHT: Fitted into Mustang serial #2, this 170-ci inline six-cylinder engine delivered 101 horsepower. When it first came out, the Mustang used a generator and changed to an alternator when the fastback model came out in 1965.

Every 5.4L DOHC V-8 engine used in the 2000 Cobra R was signed by the craftsman that assembled it. A massive plenum sat atop the aluminum powe plant and helped it crank out 390 horsepower.

While the 1978 Mustang II King Cobra gave every appearance of an old school muscle car, the 3.2L V-8 under the decal-covered hood could deliver only 139 horsepower, which was not quite enough to threaten a Boss 302.

One of LAPD's finest inspects the huge 428-ci Cobra Jet engine shoehorned into the1970 Shelby GT 500. With its 335 horsepower, the 3,850-pound vehicle had a top speed of 130 miles per hour.

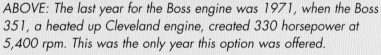

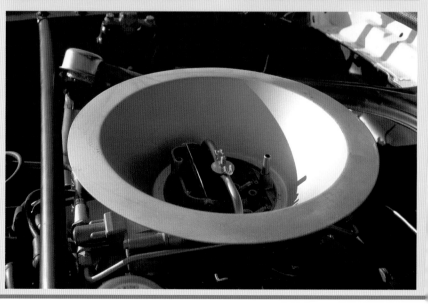

ABOVE: The last year for the Boss engine was 1971, when the Boss 351, a heated up Cleveland engine, created 330 horsepower at 5,400 rpm. This was the only year this option was offered.

TOP RIGHT: Born of the need to win in the Trans-Am series, the 1970 Boss 302 was underrated by the factory at only 290 horsepower. In reality, the high-revving powerplant made at least 350 horses.

CENTER: In 1996, Mustang performance was spelled C-O-B-R-A. With its aluminum block and heads, the 4.6L DOHC V-8 spun quickly enough to register 305 horsepower at 5,800 rpm.

RIGHT: Like a huge funnel, the air plenum sitting on top of the GT 350R helped the 289-ci V-8 make upwards of 350 horsepower. This track-only series produced only 36 vehicles.

Only one V-8 was on the Mustang menu in 1987, a 5.0L V-8 that charted at 225 horsepower. The use of electronic fuel injection helped reduce emissions and allowed for a healthy dose of power.

Bolting on a Paxton belt-driven supercharger onto the 306 horsepower 289-ci V-8 in the 1967 Shelby GT 350 raised the output by approximately 100 horsepower an added an "S" behind the GT 350 script on the rocker sill stripe.

Shelby installed the powerful 428-ci Cobra Jet engine into the GT 500 late in the 1968 model year and called it a GT 500KR. Factory rated at only 335 horsepower, it would unleash a flood of torque at very low rpm's and crest at 440 foot-pounds.

When the Mustang debuted, two V-8 engines were offered; the popular 289-ci mill and the frugal 260-ci version. With 164 horsepower, it used an Autolite two-barrel carburetor.

1986

Ford upgraded the 5.0L V-8 with a sophisticated multi-port fuel injection system. Carburetors were now a thing of the past. Once the engineers worked out the first-year kinks, the 5.0L horsepower rating moved to a respectable 225 in 1987.

1994 Mustang Cobra Coupe

The 302-ci V-8 featured cast aluminum intake manifolds and sequential electronic fuel injection. Cast aluminum alloy pistons fired inside cast-iron cylinder heads and engine block. Horsepower was rated at 240. Transmission was the manual T-5 with overdrive and limited slip differential.

1995

This was the last year for the faithful 5.0L V-8. The Windsor-based engine first appeared in 1964.

1996

The 4.6L DOHC all-alloy engine was introduced this year. The new hand-assembled powerplant used four valves per cylinder and dual overhead camshafts.

The new 305 horsepower SVT Mustang Cobra V-8 was fitted with a double-overhead cam and four valves per cylinder. The block, intake manifold, and four-valve heads were aluminum. The engine was similar in size to the venerable 351 Cleveland V-8, but the latest version was several hundred pounds lighter.

The overall efficiency was greatly improved because the engine had been designed for computerized engine management and fuel injection.

Another difference over previous engines was the way accessories were handled. The alternator, air-conditioning compressor, and power steering pump are bolted directly to the block. In the past mounting brackets added weight and vibration.

To build the engine, Ford used the best powerplant technology the world had to offer. The alloy block was cast by Teksid of Italy. The German company Gerlach Germany did the forging, and Ford's Canadian Windsor plant managed machining and finish work.

The Niche Line and the Cobra engine

A working production line can churn out 2,200 engines per hour. To build a high performance racing inspired engine, Ford prefers to slow it down a little. The Niche line was located at Ford's Romeo, Michigan, engine assembly plant.

Durable, lightweight, and strong, the 289-ci V-8 fitted into the 1966 Mustang delivered 225-horsepower in its standard, four-barrel carburetor configuration. A two-barrel version made 200 horses, while the hot K-code growled out 271.

So large it required "modifications" (hammer blows) to the shock towers to slip into the engine bay, the 1969 Boss 429 was a detuned racing engine that blasted out 370 horsepower. With a larger carburetor and big headers, the engine could easily make 500-plus horsepower.

With engine building expertise from Krause of Germany and Thyssen Production Systems of Michigan, Ford added a $3.4 million engine production facility. The 10-station line combined state-of-the-art computer-aided machinery and hand assembly.

Working in specially trained two-person teams, Ford can build a complete working engine in just over an hour. Each person on the line knows about every bolt and nut on the 4.6 Cobra engine.

When the engine is ready to leave the Niche Line, a special Mustang Cobra Engine decal is placed on the passenger side cam cover of the engine. The last step is the signature on the decal.

For the economy-minded buyer in 1966, Ford offered the Mustang Sprint, a frugal 200-ci single-barrel inline six-cylinder model. Chrome air cleaner housing and hand-applied pinstripes were part of the option package.

Like Cobras before, the 2002 model's 4.6L engine is hand-signed by the crew that built it. Engine management computers and forced induction systems allowed Ford engineers to increase power without enlarging the engine's displacement.

For the first time in 22 years, the Mustang was available with a functional Shaker hood scoop on the 2003 Mach 1. With outside air flowing into the induction system, the 4.6L DOHC V-8 was rated at 302 horsepower and 320 foot-pounds of torque.

Installing an external oil cooler in front of the radiator was part of the modifications made to transform 428 Cobra Jet into a Super Cobra Jet in the 1969 Shelby GT 500.

Improved engine management enabled Ford engineers to extract 320 horsepower from the 4.6L DOHC V-8 in the 1999 Mustang Cobra. The base price for a Cobra coupe started at $27,470.

Even though the 1966 Shelby GT 350H was available at select Hertz rental offices, the identical 305 horsepower 289-ci V-8 found in the regular GT 350 was under the long hood of the exciting rental car. It only took $17 a day and 17 cents a mile to awaken Walter Mitty.

Fitting the 428-ci Cobra Jet engine in the 1970 Mach 1 proved a challenge, as the distance between the front shock absorber towers left very little room between the cylinder heads and suspension components.

The fuel-injected 1984 Turbo GT had a compression ratio of 8.0:1, and maximum power was 145 horsepower at 4,000 rpm. The 2.3L engine housed 3.45:1 gears in the differential.

As part of a regional sales effort, Ford sold High Country Special Mustangs in Colorado in the mid-1960s. The majority were equipped with the 289-ci V-8, rated at 195 horsepower. Wires running from the hood are connected to remote turn signal indicator lamps located in the hood.

Mustang Production

Signalflare Red
Silver Blue
Silver Blue Metallic
Silver Frost
Springtime Yellow
Tahoe Turquoise
Vintage Burgundy
Wimbledon White

1966

Shelby Production

GT 350	1,368
GT 350 convertible	4
GT 350H Hertz	1,001
GT 350 Race	4
Total	2,377

Retail Price

GT 350	$4,428

Exterior colors

Candy Apple Red
Ivy Green
Raven Black
Sapphire Blue
Wimbledon White

1967

Convertible, standard	38,751
Convertible, bench seats	1,209
Convertible, luxury	4,848
Coupe, standard	325,853
Coupe, bench seats	8,190
Coupe, luxury	22,228
Fastback, standard	53,651
Fastback, luxury	17,391
Total	472,121

Retail prices

Convertible, standard	$2,898
Coupe, standard	$2,461
Fastback, standard	$2,692

Exterior Colors

Acapulco Blue
Anniversary Gold
Arcadian Blue

Aspen Gold
Blue Bonnet
Bright Red
Brittany Blue
Burnt Amber
Candy Apple Red
Clearwater Aqua
Columbine Blue
Dark Moss Green
Diamond Blue
Diamond Green
Dusk Rose
Frost Turquoise
Lavender
Lime Gold
Nightmist Blue
Pebble Beige
Playboy Pink
Raven Black
Sauterne Gold
Silver Frost
Springtime Yellow
Timberline Green
Vintage Burgundy
Wimbledon White

1967

Shelby Production

GT 350	1,175
GT 500	2,048
Special	2
Total	3,225

Exterior Colors

Brittany Blue
Bronze Metallic
Dark Blue Metallic
Dark Moss Green
Lime Green
Medium Metallic Gray
Raven Black
Red
Silver Frost
Wimbledon White

1968

Convertible, standard	22,037

179

Convertible, deluxe	3,339
Coupe, standard	233,472
Coupe, bench seats	6,113
Coupe, deluxe, bench	9,009
Fastback standard	33,585
Fastback bench seats	1,079
Fastback deluxe	7,661
Fastback deluxe bench seat	256
Total	317,404

Retail Prices

Convertible, standard	$2,814
Coupe, standard	$2,578
Fastback, standard	$2,689

Exterior Colors

Acapulco Blue
Brittany Blue
Candy Apple Red
Gulfstream Aqua
Highland Green
Lime Gold
Meadowlark Yellow
Pebble Beige
Presidential Blue
Royal Maroon
Seafoam Green
Sunlit Gold
Tahoe Turquoise
Wimbledon White

1968

Shelby Production

GT 350 Convertible	404
GT 500 Convertible	402
GT 500KR Convertible	318
GT 350 Fastback	1,253
GT 500 Fastback	1,140
GT 500 KR Fastback	933
GT 500 Special	1
Total	4,451

Retail prices

GT 350 Convertible	$4,238
GT 500 Convertible	$4,438
GT 500KR Convertible	$4,594
GT 350 Fastback	$4,116
GT 500 Fastback	$4,317
GT 500KR Fastback	$4,472

Exterior Colors

Candy Apple Red
Dark Blue Metallic
Dark Green Metallic
Gold Metallic
Lime Green Metallic
Medium Blue Metallic
Meadowlark Yellow
Orange
Raven Black
Wimbledon White

1969

Convertible, standard	11,307
Convertible, deluxe	3,439
Coupe, standard	118,613
Coupe, bench seats	4,131
Coupe, deluxe	5,210
Coupe, deluxe, bench	504
Coupe, Grande	22,182
Fastback, standard	56,022
Fastback, deluxe	5,958
Fastback, Mach 1	72,458
Boss 302	1,628
Boss 429	869
Total	299,824

Retail Prices

Convertible, standard	$2,832
Coupe, standard	$2,618
Grande coupe	$2,849
Fastback, standard	$2,618
Fastback, Mach 1	$3,122

Exterior Colors

Acapulco Blue
Aztec Aqua
Black Jade
Calypso Coral
Candy Apple Red
Champagne Gold
Gulfstream Aqua
Indian Fire Red
Lime Gold
Meadowlark Yellow

New Lime
Pastel Gray
Raven Black
Royal Maroon
Silver Jade
Wimbledon White
Winter Blue

1969-1970

Shelby Production
789 Unsold 1969 models received new badges and carried over as 1970 models.

Production
GT 350 Convertible	194
GT 500 Convertible	335
GT 350 Fastback	935
GT 500 Fastback	1,536
GT 500 Fastback Hertz	150
Special	3
Total	3,153

Retail prices
GT 350 Convertible	$4,753
GT 500 Convertible	$5,027
GT 350 Fastback	$4,434
GT 500 Fastback	$4,709

Exterior Colors
Acapulco Blue
Black Jade
Candy Apple Red
Grabber Blue
Grabber Geen
Grabber Orange
Grabber Yellow
Gulfstream Aqua
Pastel Gray
Royal Maroon
Silver Jade

1970
Convertible	7,673
Coupe	82,569
Coupe, Grande	13,581
Fastback	45,934
Fastback Mach 1	40,970

Boss 302	7,013
Boss 429	499
Total	198,239

Retail Prices
Convertible	$3,025
Coupe, standard	$2,721
Coupe, Grande, standard	$2,926
Fastback, standard	$2,771
Fastback Mach 1 standard	$3,271
Boss 302	$3,720
Boss 429	$4,928

Exterior Colors
Bright Gold Metallic
Calypso Coral
Dark Ivy Green Metallic
Grabber Blue
Grabber Green
Grabber Orange
Light Ivy Yellow
Medium Blue Metallic
Medium Gold Metallic
Medium Lime Metallic
Pastel Blue
Raven Black
Red
Silver Blue Metallic
Yellow
Wimbledon White

1971
Convertible	6,121
Coupe	65,696
Coupe, Grande	17,406
Fastback	23,956
Fastback, Mach 1	36,499
Boss 351	1,806
Total	151,484

Retail Prices
Convertible, standard	$3,227
Coupe, standard	$2,911
Coupe, Grande, standard	$3,117
Fastback, standard	$2,973
Fastback, Mach 1	$3,268
Boss 351	$4,124

Exterior Colors

Bright Red
Dark Ivy Green Metallic
Gold Metallic
Gold Glamour
Grabber Blue
Grabber Green Metallic
Grabber Lime
Grabber Yellow
Light Gold
Light Pewter Metal
Maroon Metallic
Medium Brown Metallic
Medium Green Metallic
Medium Yellow Gold
Pastel Blue
Raven Black
Silver Blue Metallic
Wimbledon White

1972

Convertible	6,321
Coupe	57,350
Coupe, Grande	18,045
Fastback	16,622
Fastback, Mach 1	27,675
Total	125,813

Retail Prices

Convertible, standard	$2,965	
Coupe, standard	$2,679	
Coupe, Grande, standard		$2,865
Fastback	$2,736	
Fastback, Mach 1, standard		$3,003

Exterior Colors

Bright Blue Metallic
Bright Lime
Bright Red
Dark Green Metallic
Gold Glow
Grabber Blue
Ivy Glow
Light Blue
Light Pewter Metallic
Maroon
Medium Bright Yellow
Medium Brown Metallic
Medium Green Metallic

Medium Yellow Gold
Wimbledon White

1973

Convertible	11,835
Coupe	51,480
Coupe Grande	25,274
Fastback	10,820
Fastback, Mach I	35,440
Total	134,867

Retail Prices

Convertible, standard	$3,102	
Coupe, standard	$2,760	
Coupe, Grande, standard		$2,946
Fastback, standard	$2,820	
Fastback, Mach I, standard		$3,088

Exterior colors

Blue Glow
Ivy Glow
Bright Red
Dark Green Metallic
Gold Glow
Ivy Glow
Light Blue
Medium Aqua
Medium Blue Metallic
Medium Bright Yellow
Medium Brown Metallic
Medium Copper Metallic
Medium Green Metallic
Medium Yellow Gold
Saddle Bronze Metallic
Wimbledon White

1974

Coupe	177,671
Coupe, Ghia	89,477
Hatchback	74,799
Hatchback, Mach 1	44,046
Total	385,993

Retail Prices

Coupe, standard	$3,134
Coupe, Ghia, standard	$3,480
Hatchback, standard	$3,328
Hatchback, Mach 1, standard	$3,674

Exterior colors
Bright Green Gold Metallic
Bright Red
Dark Red
Ginger Glow
Green Glow
Light Blue
Medium Bright Blue Metallic
Medium Copper Metallic
Medium Lime Yellow
Medium Yellow Gold
Pearl White
Saddle Bronze Metallic
Silver Metallic
Tan Glow

1975

Coupe	85,155
Coupe, Ghia	52,320
Hatchback	30,038
Hatchback, Mach 1	21,062
Total	188,575

Retail Prices

Coupe, standard	$3,529
Coupe, Ghia, standard	$3,938
Hatchback, standard	$3,818
Hatchback, Mach 1,standard	$4,188

Exterior Colors
Black
Bright Blue Metallic
Bright Red
Bright Yellow
Dark Brown Metallic
Dark Red
Dark Yellow Green Metallic
Green Glow
Light Green
Medium Copper Metallic
Pastel Blue
Polar White
Silver Blue Glow
Silver Metallic
Tan Glow

1976

Coupe	78,508
Coupe, Ghia	37,515
Hatchback	62,312
Hatchback, Mach I	9,232
Total	187,567

Retail Prices

Coupe, standard	$3,525
Coupe, Ghia, standard	$3,859
Hatchback, standard	$3,781
Hatchback, Mach I,standard	$4,209

Exterior Colors
Black
Bright Blue Metallic
Bright Red
Bright Yellow
Dark Brown Metallic
Dark Red
Dark Yellow Green Metallic
Light Green
Medium Chestnut Metallic
Medium Ivy Bronze Metallic
Polar White
Silver Blue Glow
Silver Metallic
Tan Glow

Tu-Tone Color Combinations
Cream/Medium Gold Metallic
White/Bright Red
White/Bright Blue Metallic

1977

Coupe	67,783
Coupe, Ghia	29,510
Hatchback	49,161
Hatchback, Mach 1	6,719
Total	153,173

Retail Prices

Coupe, standard	$3,678
Coupe, Ghia, standard	$4,096
Hatchback, standard	$3,877
Hatchback, Mach 1,standard	$4,332

Exterior Colors
Black
Bright Aqua Glow
Bright Red

Bright Saddle Metallic
Bright Yellow
Cream
Dark Brown Metallic
Golden Glow
Light Aqua Metallic
Medium Emerald Glow
Orange
Polar White
Tan

Tu-Tone Color Combinations
Cream/Medium Gold Metallic
White/Light Aqua Metallic
White/Bright Red

1978
Coupe	81,304
Coupe, Ghia	34,730
Hatchback	68,408
Hatchback, Mach 1	7,968
Total	192,410

Retail Prices
Coupe, standard	$3,824
Coupe, Ghia, standard	$4,242
Hatchback, standard	$4,088
Hatchback, Mach 1, standard	$4,523

Exterior Colors
Aqua Glow
Aqua Metallic
Black
Bright Red
Bright Yellow
Chamois Glow
Dark Brown Metallic
Dark Jade Metallic
Dark Midnight Blue
Light Chamois
Medium Chestnut Metallic
Polar White
Silver Metallic
Tangerine

Tu-Tone Color Combinations
Bright Aqua/Metallic White
Bright Red/Black
Bright Red/White
Bright Yellow/Black

Dark Jade Metallic/White
Light Aqua Metallic/White
Light Chamois/Medium Chestnut Metallic
Silver Metallic/Black
Silver Metallic/Bright Red
Tangerine/White
White/Aqua Metallic
White/Black
White/Bright Red

1979
Coupe	156,666
Coupe, Ghia	56,351
Hatchback	120,535
Hatchback, Ghia	36,384
Total	369,936

Retail Prices
Coupe, standard	$4,494
Coupe, Ghia, standard	$5,064
Hatchback, standard	$4,828
Hatchback,Ghia, standard	$5,216

Exterior colors
Black
Bright Blue
Bright Red
Bright Yellow
Dark Jade Metallic
Light Chamois
Light Medium Blue
Medium Blue Glow
Medium Chestnut Metallic
Medium Gray Metallic
Medium Vaquero Gold
Polar White
Red Glow
Silver Metallic
Tangerine

Tu-Tone Color Combinations
Light Medium Blue/Bright Blue
Silver Metallic/Medium Gray Metallic

1980
Coupe	128,893
Coupe, Ghia	23,647
Hatchback	98,497

Hatchback, Ghia   20,285
Total   271,322

Retail Prices
Coupe $5,338
Coupe, Ghia, standard $5,823
Hatchback, standard $5,816
Hatchback, Ghia, standard $5,935

Exterior Colors
Bittersweet Glow
Black
Bright Bittersweet
Bright Blue
Bright Caramel
Bright Red
Bright Yellow
Chamois Glow
Dark Chamois Metallic
Dark Cordovan Metallic
Light Medium Blue
Medium Blue Glow
Medium Gray Metallic
Polar White
Silver Metallic

Tu-Tone Color Combinations
Bittersweet Glow/Dark Cordovan Metallic
Bright Bittersweet/Dark Cordovan Metallic
Chamois Glow/Dark Chamois Metallic
Dark Chamois Metallic/Chamois Glow
Dark Cordovan Metallic/Bittersweet Glow
Light Medium Blue/Bright Blue
Polar White/Bittersweet Glow
Polar White/Bright Yellow
Silver Metallic/Dark Cordovan Metallic
Silver Metallic/Medium Gray Metallic

1981
Coupe   77,458
Coupe, Ghia   13,422
Hatchback   77,399
Hatchback, Ghia   14,273
Total   182,552

Retail Prices
Coupe, standard $5,897
Hatchback, standard $6,566
Hatchback, Ghia standard $6,786

Exterior Colors
Black
Bittersweet Glow
Bright Bittersweet
Bright Red
Bright Yellow
Dark Brown Metallic
Dark Cordovan Metallic
Light Pewter Metallic
Medium Blue Glow
Medium Pewter Metallic
Midnight Blue Metallic
Pastel Chamois
Polar White
Red

Tu-Tone Color Combinations
Bittersweet Glow/Black
Bright Bittersweet/Black
Bright Red/Black
Bright Yellow/Black
Dark Cordovan Metallic/Black
Light Pewter Metallic/Black
Medium Pewter Metallic/Light Pewter Metallic
Pastel Chamois/Black
Polar White/Bittersweet Glow
Red/Black
Red/Polar White

1982
Coupe   45,316
Coupe GLX   5,828
Hatchback   69,348
Hatchback GLX   9,926
Total   130,418

Retail Prices
Coupe, standard $6,346
Coupe, GLX standard $6,980
Hatchback, standard $6,979
Hatchback, GLX, standard $7,101

Exterior Colors
Bittersweet Glow
Black
Bright Red
Dark Blue Metallic
Dark Cordovan Metallic

Dark Curry Brown Metallic
Medium Blue Glow
Medium Gray Metallic
Medium Vanilla
Medium Yellow
Pastel Vanilla
Polar White
Red
Silver Metallica

Tu-Tone Color Combinations
Bittersweet Glow/Black
Bright Red/Black
Dark Blue Metallic/Black
Dark Blue Metallic/Medium Blue Glow
Dark Cordovan Metallic/Bittersweet Glow
Dark Cordovan Metallic/Black
Medium Blue Glow/Black
Medium Gray Metallic/Black
Medium Gray Metallic/Silver Metallic
Medium Vanilla/Black
Medium Vanilla/Pastel Vanilla
Medium Yellow/Black
Pastel Vanilla/Black
Polar White/Black
Red/Black
Silver Metallic/Black

1983

Convertible	23,438
Coupe	33,201
Hatchback	64,234
Total	120,873

Retail prices

Convertible, standard	$12,467
Coupe, standard	$ 6,727
Hatchback, standard	$7,439

Exterior Colors
Black
Bright Bittersweet
Bright Red
Dark Academy Blue Metallic
Dark Walnut Metallic
Desert Tan Glow
Light Academy Blue Glow
Light Desert Tan
Medium Charcoal Metallic
Medium Yellow

Midnight Blue Metallic
Polar White
Red
Silver White

1984

Convertible	17,600
Coupe	37,680
Hatchback	86,200
Total	141,480

20th Anniversary Special Editions

Convertible Turbo GT	104
Convertible 5.0L GT	1,213
VIP Convertible	16
Canadian	246
Hatchback 5.0L GT	3,333
Hatchback Turbo GT	350
Total	5,262

Retail Prices

Convertible, standard	$11,840
Coupe, standard	$ 7, 089
Hatchback, standard	$7,260

Exterior Colors
Black
Bright Canyon Red
Bright Copper Glow
Dark Academy Blue Metallic
Dark Charcoal Metallic
Desert Tan Glow
Light Academy Blue Glow
Light Desert Tan
Medium Canyon Red Glow
Oxford White
Silver Metallic

1985

Convertible	15, 110
Coupe	56,781
Hatchback	84,623
Total	156,514

Retail Prices

Convertible, standard	$12, 237
Coupe, standard	$ 6,989
Hatchback, standard	$7,509

Exterior Colors
Black
Canyon Red
Dark Sable
Jalapeno Red
Medium Charcoal
Medium Regatta Blue
Oxford Gray
Oxford White
Pastel Regatta Blue
Sand Beige
Silver

1986

Convertible	22, 946
Coupe	83,774
Hatchback	117,690
Total	224,410

Retail Prices

Convertible, standard	$13,214
Coupe, standard	$7,420
Hatchback, standard	$7,974

Exterior Colors
Black
Bright Red
Dark Clove Metallic
Dark Gray Metallic
Dark Sage
Dark Sage Metallic
Light Regatta Blue Metallic
Medium Canyon Red Metallic
Oxford White
Sand Beige
Shadow Blue Metallic
Silver Metallic

1987

Convertible	32, 074
Coupe	43, 257
Hatchback	94,441
Total	169,772

Retail Prices Standard

Convertible	$13,052
Coupe	$8,271
Hatchback	$8,690

Exterior Colors
Black
Bright Regatta Blue Metallic
Dark Clove Metallic
Dark Gray Metallic
Dark Shadow Blue Metallic
Light Gray
Medium Cabernet
Medium Shadow Blue Metallic
Medium Yellow
Oxford White
Sand Beige
Scarlet Red

1988

Convertible	32,074
Coupe	53,221
Hatchback	125,930
Total	211,225

Retail Prices Standard

Convertible	$13,702
Coupe	$8,835
Hatchback	$9,341

Exterior Colors
Almond
Black
Bright Red
Bright Regatta Blue Metallic
Cabernet Red
Dark Gray Metallic
Deep Shadow Blue Metallic
Light Gray
Medium Shadow Blue Metallic
Oxford White
Tropical Yellow

1989

Convertible	42,244
Coupe	50,560
Hatchback	116,965
Total	209,769

Retail Prices Standard

Convertible	$14,140
Coupe	$9,050
Hatchback	$9, 556

Exterior Colors

Almond
Black
Bright Red
Bright Regatta Blue Metallic
Cabernet Red
Dark Gray Metallic
Deep Shadow Blue Metallic
Light Gray
Medium Shadow Blue Metallic
Oxford White
Tropical Yellow

1990

Convertible	26,958
Coupe	22,503
Hatchback	78,728
Total	128,189

Retail Prices Standard

Convertible	$14,810
Coupe	$9,753
Hatchback	$10,259

Exterior Colors

Black
Bright Red
Bright Yellow
Cabernet Red
Crystal Blue
Deep Emerald Green
Deep Titanium
Light Titanium
Oxford White
Twilight Blue
Wild Strawberry

1991

Convertible	21,512
Coupe	19,447
Hatchback	57,777
Total	98,737

Retail Prices Standard

Convertible	$16,767
Coupe	$10,702
Hatchback	$11,208

Exterior Colors

Black
Bright Red
Deep Emerald Green
Light Crystal Blue
Medium Red
Medium Titanium
Oxford White
Titanium Frost
Twilight Blue
Wild Strawberry

1992

Convertible	23,470
Coupe	15,717
Hatchback	40,093
Total	79,280

Retail Prices Standard

Convertible	$16,899
Coupe	$10,125
Hatchback	$10,721

Exterior Colors

Bimini Blue
Black
Bright Red
Deep Emerald Green
Medium Red
Medium Titanium
Oxford White
Titanium Frost
Twilight Blue
Ultra Blue
Wild Strawberry

1993

Convertible	27,300
Coupe	24,851
Hatchback	57,084
Cobra Hatchback	4,993
Total	114,228

Retail Prices Standard

Convertible	$17,988
Coupe	$11,159
Hatchback	$11,664

Exterior Colors

Black
Bright Blue
Bright Calypso Green
Bright Red
Electric Red
Reef Blue
Royal Blue
Silver
Vibrant White

1994

Cobra Convertible	1,000
Convertible 3.8L	18,333
Convertible GT	25,381
Cobra Coupe	5,009
Coupe GT	30,592
Coupe 3.8L	42,883
Hatchback	57,084
Total	123,198

Retail Prices Standard

Cobra Convertible	$25,605
Convertible GT	$21,790
Convertible	$20,160
Cobra Coupe	$21,300
Coupe GT	$17,280
Coupe	$13,365

Exterior Colors

Black
Bright Blue
Canary Yellow
Crystal White
Deep Forest Green
Iris
Laser Red
Opal Frost
Rio Red
Teal
Vibrant Red

1995

Convertible, standard	48, 264
Cobra Convertible	1,003
Coupe	137,722
Cobra Coupe	4,005

Total	190,994

Retail Prices Standard

Cobra Convertible	$25,605
Convertible	$20,995
Cobra Coupe	$21,300
Coupe	$14,530

Exterior Colors

Black
Bright Blue
Canary Yellow
Crystal White
Deep Forest Green
Laser Red
Opal Frost
Rio Red
Sapphire Blue
Teal
Vibrant Red

1996

Cobra Convertible	2,510
Convertible	15,246
GT Convertible	17,917
Cobra Coupe	7,496
Coupe	61,187
GT Coupe	31,624
Total	135,980

Retail Prices Standard

Cobra Convertible	$27,580
Convertible GT	$23,495
Convertible	$21,060
Cobra Coupe	$24,810
Cobra GT	$17,610
Coupe	$15,180

Exterior Colors

Black
Bright Tangerine
Deep Forest Green
Deep Violet
Laser Red
Moonlight Blue
Mystic
Pacific Green
Rio Red

Opal Frost
Crystal White

1997

Cobra Convertible	3,088
Convertible GT	11,413
Convertible	11,606
Cobra Coupe	6,961
GT Coupe	18,464
Coupe	56,812
Total	108,344

Retail Prices

Cobra Convertible	$28,135
Convertible GT	$24,510
Convertible	$21,280
Cobra Coupe	$25,335
Coupe GT	$18,525
Coupe	$15,880

Exterior Colors

Autumn Orange
Aztec Gold
Black
Crystal White
Deep Forest Green
Deep Violet
Laser Red
Moonlight Blue
Pacific Green
Rio Red

1998

Cobra Convertible	3,480
Convertible GT	17,024
Convertible	21,254
Cobra Coupe	5,174
Coupe GT	28,789
Coupe	99,801
Total	175,522

Retail Prices Standard

Cobra Convertible	$28,510
Convertible GT	$24,150
Convertible	$20,650
Cobra Coupe	$25,710
Coupe GT	$20,150
Coupe	$16,150

Exterior Colors

Atlantic Blue
Autumn Orange
Black
Bright Atlantic Blue
Chrome Yellow
Crystal White
Dark Green Satin
Laser Red
Pacific Green
Performance Red
Rio Red
Silver

1999

Cobra Convertible	4,055
Convertible GT	13,699
Convertible	19,299
Cobra Coupe	4.040
Coupe GT	19,634
Coupe	73,180
Total	133,907

Retail Prices Standard

Cobra Convertible	$31,470
Convertible GT	$24,870
Convertible	$21,070
Cobra Coupe	$27,470
Coupe GT	$20,870
Coupe	$16,470

Exterior Colors

Atlantic Blue
Black
Bright Atlantic Blue
Chrome Yellow
Crystal White
Dark Green Satin
Electric Green
Laser Red
Performance Red
Rio Red
Silver

2000

Cobra Convertible	100
Convertible GT	20,224
Convertible	41,368

Cobra Coupe	354
Coupe GT	32,321
Coupe	121,026
Total	215,393

Retail Prices Standard

Cobra Convertible	$31,605
Convertible GT	$25,270
Convertible	$21,370
Cobra Coupe	$27,605
Coupe GT	$21,015
Coupe	$16,520

Exterior Colors

Amazon Green
Atlantic Blue
Black
Bright Atlantic Blue
Crystal White
Electric Green
Laser Red
Performance Red
Silver
Sunburst Gold

2001

Standard Coupe	75,321
Convertible	30,399
GT Coupe	32,511
GT Convertible	18,336
Cobra Coupe	3,867
Cobra Convertible	3,384

Retail Prices

Standard Coupe	$16,805
Deluxe Convertible	$22,220
GT Deluxe Coupe	$22,440
GT Premium Convertible	$27,850

2002

Coupe
Convertible
GT Coupe
GT Convertible

Retail Prices

Coupe	$17,220
Convertible	$22,540
GT Coupe	$22,760
GT Convertible	$28,185

2003

Coupe
Coupe Deluxe
Coupe Premium
GT Deluxe
GT Premium
GT Premium Convertible
Mach I
SVT Cobra
SVT Cobra Convertible

Retail Prices

Coupe	$17,695
Coupe Deluxe	$18,425
Coupe Premium	$23,395
GT Deluxe	$23,680
GT Premium	$24,840
GT Premium Convertible	$29,155
Mach I	$28,680
SVT Cobra	$33,440
SVT Cobra Convertible	$37,780

Exterior Colors

Azure Blue
Sonic Blue Metallic
True Blue Metallic
Silver Metallic
Black
Dark Shadow Gray Metallic
Torch Red
Fire Red Metallic
Tropical Green Metallic
Oxford White
Zinc Yellow